T0304048

ROUTLEDGE LIBRARY EDITIONS:
INDUSTRIAL RELATIONS

Volume 37

WAGE REGULATION UNDER THE STATUTE OF ARTIFICERS

ROUTLEDGE LIBRARY EDITIONS:
INDUSTRIAL RELATIONS

Volume 37

WAGE REGULATION UNDER
THE STATUTE OF ARTIFICERS

WAGE REGULATION UNDER THE STATUTE OF ARTIFICERS

R. KEITH KELSALL

Routledge
Taylor & Francis Group

LONDON AND NEW YORK

First published in 1938 by Methuen & Co. Ltd.

This edition first published in 2025
by Routledge
4 Park Square, Milton Park, Abingdon, Oxon OX14 4RN

and by Routledge
605 Third Avenue, New York, NY 10158

Routledge is an imprint of the Taylor & Francis Group, an informa business

British Library Cataloguing in Publication Data
A catalogue record for this book is available from the British Library

ISBN: 978-1-032-81770-5 (Set)
ISBN: 978-1-032-81458-2 (Volume 37) (hbk)
ISBN: 978-1-032-81473-5 (Volume 37) (pbk)
ISBN: 978-1-003-49996-1 (Volume 37) (ebk)

DOI: 10.4324/9781003499961

Publisher's Note
The publisher has gone to great lengths to ensure the quality of this reprint but points out that some imperfections in the original copies may be apparent.

Disclaimer
The publisher has made every effort to trace copyright holders and would welcome correspondence from those they have been unable to trace.

WAGE REGULATION UNDER
THE STATUTE OF ARTIFICERS

by

R. KEITH KELSALL, M.A.

LECTURER IN ECONOMICS AT
UNIVERSITY COLLEGE, HULL

METHUEN & CO. LTD. LONDON
36 Essex Street Strand W.C.2

First published in 1938

PREFACE

SO many economic historians have, in the past, been attracted by the Elizabethan labour code as a subject of study, that it may be as well to explain what gap this book is intended to fill. Briefly, it is hoped to provide a rather fuller treatment of wage assessment under the Statute of Artificers than has hitherto been published. In doing this my indebtedness to Professor Tawney's work will be constantly apparent—indeed, so far as suggestive ideas are concerned, it would be hard to improve upon his masterly analysis, published in *Vierteljahrschrift für Sozial-und Wirtschaftsgeschichte* in 1914. What one can perhaps do, however, is to bring forward additional evidence on many different points, which may lead to changes in emphasis. This additional evidence comes, in the main, from sessions records. A large number of these has been published since the war, several since the appearance of volume three of Lipson's *Economic History of England* in 1931. (Lipson, incidentally, apparently overlooked one or two that were published long before that date, notably the *Somerset Quarter Sessions Records*.) Full use has been made of this new printed material, but an attempt has also been made to utilize some of the unpublished records, most of which will not be printed for many years if, indeed, they are ever published.

The scope of the present study is at once narrower and wider than the title would suggest. Thus on the one hand, it has already been satisfactorily established that there was little novelty about Elizabethan labour legislation, that precedents both national and local lay to hand. Again, the full significance of the Gloucestershire clothiers' eighteenth century struggle against wage assessment, leading to the exemption of the woollen industry, and of the early nineteenth century efforts to revive assessment, has been brought out elsewhere. To neither of these questions is anything more than incidental reference made in the following pages, not because their importance is not appreciated, but simply because the records examined throw no additional light upon them, and mere repetition of what has already been so well said seems pointless. For the same reason, it has not been thought necessary to recapitulate what is known regarding poor law practices, or the functions of justices, high constables and petty constables, or the development of industrial organization and similar questions. The relevance of this knowledge to the subject under consideration is not, of course, denied; but those who read this book can be relied upon to fit it into the appropriate setting for themselves, without the reminders which would be necessary in a general text. On the other hand, the present study embraces not merely the assessment of wages itself, but other closely allied parts of the Elizabethan labour code. Naturally, some selection had to be made, and the group of subjects centring on apprenticeship was excluded.

Finally, there are three points in particular on which I anticipate criticism, where I should like to say a few words in defence of the procedure here adopted. The first is that more use has not been made of early treatises on the practice of justices, which Dr. Putnam has done so much to make more readily available. In this book we are, in the main, concerned with the administration of an Elizabethan statute, and the offences, penalties and procedure to be followed are, on the whole, clear enough. True, there are doubts—as to the exact functioning of the high constable's "petty sessions", for instance—but these and similar difficulties are of a type which can only, in my opinion, be resolved by a close examination of sessions records in different parts of the country, and on which general treatises shed, at best, an uncertain light. Nor, according to Professor Tawney, should too much reliance be placed on the evidence of Lambard and the others as to the regularity, in different periods, of the practice of assessment.

Secondly, some will no doubt feel that too much space is devoted, in what follows, to irrelevant detail as, for instance, in the discussion of the exact wording of entries in sessions minutes. It seems to me, however, that the subject under review has now reached a stage at which, before fresh advances can be made, rather careful examination of the nature of the evidence on which many of our conclusions are based is necessary. It is perhaps not generally realized, for instance, how much individual judgment sometimes enters into the apparently simple task of distinguishing an entry in sessions minutes involving reissue of the existing scale from one involving the promulgation of a new scale. In these circumstances the more collective experience (for guidance in making such judgments, and for estimating the probable error in conclusions) is made available, the better. It is for this reason among others, that I have printed as an appendix a tentative list of dates when new scales of wages were apparently drawn up. This list—though it probably contains many mistakes—both expands and corrects previous lists (such as Cunningham's and Lipson's); it is intended as a guide and nothing more.

Thirdly, it may be felt that more use should have been made of the material available, that there should have been comparison of assessed rates in the same area at different dates, and in different areas at the same date. I do not myself feel, however, that the conclusions which usually emerge from comparisons of this type—to the effect, say, that wages in the north were higher than those in the south, and that the general movement of wages was in an upward direction—quite justify the labour involved in arriving at them. In any case, the matter will presumably be gone into very fully in future volumes of the history of prices which Sir William Beveridge and his helpers are preparing. Moreover, so far as general comparisons are concerned, it is unlikely that more information can be gleaned from the existing material than has been done by Miss Hindmarsh, to whose unpublished London University thesis my attention was only drawn when the present study was virtually completed.

ACKNOWLEDGMENTS

I should like to record my indebtedness to the following persons who have helped me by granting permission to examine records, by allowing me to print material, or in other ways.

Sir William Beveridge, Miss E. M. Brown, Mr. Leonard Chubb, Mr. B. C. Duddles, Mr. J. W. F. Hill, Sir Godfrey MacDonald of the Isles, The Dowager Duchess of Norfolk, Rev. Prebendary T. F. Palmer (Somerset Record Society), Dr. S. A. Peyton, Miss M. E. Rayner, and Professor R. H. Tawney (who very kindly read the book in manuscript and made a number of helpful suggestions).

The Clerks of the Peace of the Parts of Holland and Lindsey in Lincolnshire, of Norfolk, Staffordshire, Suffolk, and the East and West Ridings of Yorkshire, and their staffs.

The Incumbents of numerous parishes in Lincolnshire and Yorkshire.

The Librarians of Canterbury, Chester, Hull, Hull University College, Ipswich, Manchester University, Norwich, Queen's College Oxford, and St. Albans, and their staffs.

The Mayor of Hedon.

The Town Clerks of Aldeburgh, Beverley, Great Grimsby, Great Yarmouth, Hertford, Hull, Ipswich, Scarborough, and Thetford, and their staffs.

CONTENTS

LIST OF ABBREVIATED REFERENCES
(For Bibliography, see page 123.)

C.R.	County Records.
E.H.R.	English Historical Review.
E.J.	Economic Journal.
Econ.H.R.	Economic History Review.
H.M.C.	Historical Manuscripts Commission.
N.R.Q.S.R.	North Riding Quarter Sessions Records.
Q.S.	Quarter Sessions.
V.C.H.	Victoria County History.
V.S.W.	Vierteljahrschrift für Sozial-und Wirt- schaftsgeschichte.
W.R.S.	West Riding Sessions.

In other cases, where a name and page only are given, the full title will be found under that name in the bibliography.

CHAPTER I

ASSESSMENTS AND REISSUES

WORKERS in the field of wage assessment labour
under one serious initial handicap, in that there is no
certainty as to where, for any particular county or borough,
the assessments themselves may be found. For the first years
of the Statute's operation, it is true, the procedure was
reasonably clear. Justices were, at Easter Sessions, to rate
wages and certify them into Chancery: if approved, they
would then be issued as Proclamations, and copies sent to
the counties of origin for distribution.[1] Although the entries
in the Privy Council Register suggest that the central
government performed its functions in this matter,[2] we are
dependent on the survival of Proclamations for most of our
knowledge regarding the rates laid down by the justices at
this period. Those Proclamations incorporating assessments
which have survived are clearly only a fraction of the
original number, and there does not seem to be much likeli-
hood of discovering more at the present time. After 1597,
however, certification into Chancery ceased to be necessary.[3] The position in the East Riding at the middle of the
seventeenth century seems, incidentally, to have been that
certification into Chancery was still believed to be necessary—the justices in 1647 ordered the Clerk of the Peace to
"certifie upp above the rates of servants wages and procure

[1] 5 Eliz. c. 4, sec. 11. The Statute is, of course, printed in full in
two readily-accessible collections of documents—Bland, 325–33, and
Tawney and Power, I, 338–50. I have followed their numbering of
the sections.
[2] E.H.R. XV, 448.
[3] 39 Eliz. c. 12.

1

proclamations thereupon according to the forme of the statute"[1]; I know of no other case, however, in which this mistake was made. The problem of locating assessments was not rendered any easier by the change in procedure. The Clerk of the Peace was, it is true, responsible for keeping the parchment rolls on which the rates decided on were engrossed. In some cases he may have kept them separately from other sessions papers,[2] in other cases they were filed in the general sessions bundles;[3] more commonly they were treated as of purely ephemeral interest, and were lost or destroyed. The absence of the parchment rolls themselves is not always, however, a sign that the rates assessed cannot be found, for several other possible sources exist. In the first place, where minutes of proceedings at Quarter Sessions were kept, an entry relating to this matter was sometimes made;[4] it was not usual, unfortunately, actually to copy the rates into the minutes, though occasionally this was done.[5] A second possible place of record was the book of sessions orders. Early researchers relied largely on this source, and were led into the error of supposing that, if no mention of assessment was included amongst the orders, no action in the matter of assessment was being taken by the justices.[6] It would be equally wrong, however, to assume that order books could safely be ignored in this connection, for in some districts the assessed rates were issued as orders,[7] whether this was a misconstruction of the terms of the Statute or not. It is worth mentioning, incidentally, that although it was originally[8] laid down that wages should be assessed at Easter Sessions, entries are sometimes found in minute or order books under later sessions, either because

[1]East Riding Q.S. Books, October 1647.
[2]This appears to have happened at Hull.
[3]Gilboy, 247.
[4]Usually amongst administrative entries, but occasionally (*e.g.* Somerset Q.S. Records III, 40, 66–7) as presentments.
[5]*E.g.* Norwich Court Books, August 1657; Holland Q.S. Minutes, Easter 1714.
[6]*Kesteven Q.S. Minutes* p. cxi.
[7]*E.J.* XXIV, 221.
[8]5 Eliz. c. 4, sec. 11.

action had been accidentally or intentionally postponed (a 1604 statute[1] authorized rating of wages at *any* general sessions), or because the clerk had forgotten to make the entry at the time. Numerous instances of this are to be found, for example, in the Ipswich and Norwich sessions records.[2]

Lack of mention of assessment in minute and order books is not, however, conclusive evidence either that an assessment was never made, or that one no longer survives. Thus in some cases minute books ignore the administrative, as distinct from the judicial, side of the justices' activities altogether;[3] while in other cases, despite the silence of the minutes, cases where rates of wages higher than those assessed were given or received show that the normal machinery must have been functioning.[4] A final possibility is that the copies transmitted to the high constables or petty constables may have survived, perhaps having been entered in petty constables' books of memoranda along with other instructions periodically received.[5] Oddly enough the distribution of large numbers of printed copies, which became quite a usual means of publication of the assessed rates in the last quarter of the seventeenth, and in the eighteenth century,[6] has not apparently meant the survival of several copies of each of the known assessments for that period. Nevertheless, a careful search of parish chests in those parts of the country where no lists of their contents have been published would probably yield a certain number of additional copies, some of which had not hitherto been recorded.

Assessments, when made, did not always apply to the entire county. Thus in those counties where each of the four sessions was duplicated (whether by adjournment or

[1] 1 Jac. I, c. 6, sec. 5.
[2] *E.g.* Ipswich Q.S. Minutes 20 Sept. 1619; Norwich Court Books, 26 Sept. 1656.
[3] The Sessions Books at Great Yarmouth are in this category.
[4] This is true of Notts. 1603–61 (Copnall, 65–6).
[5] *E.H.R.* LII, 283.
[6] *E g.* Suffolk Q.S. Order Books, April 1729: *N.R.Q.S.R.* VII, 50: and *Hertford C.R.* I, 338.

otherwise) as for instance in Suffolk, Lindsey, Holland and Kesteven, it naturally followed (and was recognized by Statute)[1] that wages were rated separately at the duplicated Easter Sessions.[2] In counties where duplication was not indulged in, it was sometimes necessary to try and achieve the same result by so wording the general assessment as to distinguish between different areas within the county. Examples of this practice are found in Buckinghamshire, where a distinction was drawn between the Vale and the Chilterns,[3] in Lancashire, where rates in the 1725 assessment were qualified by the statement "but the said county being near eighty miles in length, we think the more northern part thereof ought not to demand so much, but be content with what the custom of the country hath usually been";[4] and in Oxfordshire, where provision seems to have been made in the form of the assessment for a distinction between the North and South Divisions.[5] Assessment by divisions, though it obviously had much to commend it, has made things more difficult for research workers —when two assessments, or copies, for the same county and the same or adjacent years have survived, there is often no indication as to whether the differences between them are to be explained by careless copying, or by their being for separate divisions.[6] Another complicating factor was the existence of privileged jurisdictions within the county. An extreme case is to be found in Hertfordshire, where about one-third of the county area, the liberty of St. Albans, had

[1]39 Eliz. c. 12, sec. 2.
[2]Thus separate Suffolk assessments might be drawn up the same Easter, in the seventeenth century, for the four divisions of the county in sessions held at Beccles, Woodbridge, Ipswich and Bury. (The arrangement for duplication of sessions by adjournment in Suffolk is explained in some detail in Devreux Edgar's Diary). For the duplication of sessions in Lincolnshire, see *V.C.H. Lincs.* II, 337.
[3]*E.g. Bucks. Sessions Records* I, 227–9.
[4]*Annals of Agriculture* XXV, 312; that this represented a change of practice in Lancashire is suggested by an order of 1620 that the justices at their several sessions should rate wages within their several divisions (*Manchester Sessions*, 113).
[5]Gretton, p. lxiv.
[6]Several instances of this difficulty will be found in the list in Appendix I.

its own Quarter Sessions; in this instance the practice appears to have been to use the same *form* in drawing up a scale of wages, and at least on the one occasion for which we have information—two 1631 assessments—very similar rates.[1] Almost every county had, of course, within its area some borough with its own Quarter Sessions. Normally, this must have meant that the usual tendency for town wages in the crafts to exceed those in the surrounding country was reflected by a separate borough assessment, with appropriately higher maxima. However, the complete absence of anything directly related to the assessment of wages[2]—including mention of receiving or giving higher rates, or refusing to work for the assessed rates—amongst the reasonably full records of the borough of Hertford, suggests that in some cases the justices of these privileged areas may (by choice or by necessity) have allowed the matter of wage assessment to be dealt with at Quarter Sessions for the county as a whole.[3] The magistrates of the borough of St. Albans seem to have combined with the liberty magistrates for wage assessment purposes *inter alia*; this, at least, seems to be a reasonable interpretation of the wording of an entry in the Corporation records, dated March 1587—"it was reported that it was agreed at the Sessions holden immediately after Easter for the liberty and borough that the rate of wages . . . should remain the same as before, and this was confirmed".[4] That the grant of separate Quarter Sessions did not always and necessarily carry with it the right to assess wages separately is at least hinted at, moreover, in the wording of an assessment for the county of Lancaster in 1725—"which rates . . . we . . . have hereby ordered not to be exceeded in any part of the county . . .

[1]For similarity of *form*, compare *Hertford C.R.* I, 8–12, with Clutterbuck, I, pp. xxii-xxiv.
[2]If I am right in thinking that the 1631 assessment in the Town Clerk's custody is for a division of the *county*.
[3]*Cf. V.C.H. Herts.* III, 496—"the mayor and steward and one burgess were to be justices of the peace for the borough, but their jurisdiction seems not to have excluded that of the county magistrates".
[4]*St. Albans Corporation Records*, 17.

2

and we do think fit that in every town-corporate, within this county, this our order be by the mayor or chief officer or officers there caused to be proclaimed".[1] And even in two cases where one would have thought the right of the town to draw up its own wage-scale unlikely to be surrendered or allowed to lapse—Exeter and Oxford (an assessment for Exeter has been printed)[2]—two scholars have, without actually raising the issue, spoken as if the county rature was valid there also.[3] One would, however, be safe in suggesting that, whatever is thought about these particular cases, the normal town with its own Quarter Sessions rated wages separately. Such assessments are, unfortunately, not always easy to distinguish from assessments for a division of the county, particularly where only a truncated copy survives. The 1682 Suffolk assessment printed by Thorold Rogers,[4] for instance, may, on the evidence he gives, equally well be for Bury St. Edmunds as a borough, or for the Bury division of Suffolk.

It is, of course, of vital importance in the study of the rating of wages by the justices to be able to distinguish between a new assessment and a reissue, without alteration, of a previous scale.[5] Such a distinction is not difficult to draw where the wording used in order or minute books admits of only one interpretation. "Wages to be as last year", or "rates of wages continued" are clear enough; even "rates of wages confirmed" can safely be regarded as evidence of reissue if, in a particular series of records, the wording used in case of setting new rates is known to differ from it. Ambiguity can, however, easily arise. For one thing, how much reliance is to be placed on a date referred to in the phrasing of a subsequent reissue? In Tawney's opinion,[6] the inclusion in the 1692 sessions minutes of the

[1] *Annals of Agriculture* XXV, 312.
[2] *H.M.C. Exeter*, 50–1.
[3] Gilboy 110–11, and Hoskins, 130.
[4] *History* VI, 698–9.
[5] For the purpose of the list in the appendix, any alteration in the existing rates constitutes a new assessment.
[6] *V.S.W.* XI, 334.

phrase "the same rates of wages . . . to stand for this year
as they were appointed and settled by order of this Court
last year",[1] justified the assumption that a new North
Riding assessment had been drawn-up in 1691. Yet even
wording of a still more definite character has, on occasion,
proved misleading. We know, for example, that although
in the early years of the eighteenth century reissues for
Hertfordshire were in the form "as at Easter Sessions 1700",
the Easter 1700 assessment was itself merely a reissue of that
of 1695.[2] Another rather odd use of words is to be found in
the records of the same county. There is an order at Easter
Sessions 1687 that rates be continued, though a new assessment was drawn up at that very sessions.[3] Presumably
"continued as now assessed" is to be understood, on the
analogy of a similar case at Ipswich, "rates . . . to be continued as they are now newly assessed and appointed by
the Court".[4] It should be added, incidentally, that reissues
were, when the need arose, proclaimed or printed and distributed as if they were new assessments,[5] a circumstance
which naturally makes it even harder to distinguish the
two. From a legal point of view there was, of course, no
distinction; but this is small compensation to the student of
economic history, to whom the reissue of the existing rates
without alteration is a very different matter from a revision
of the scale.

The number of known reissues is, of course, very much
larger than the number of known new assessments—indeed
the printing of a complete list of these reissues would take up
more space than it would justify. The Kent assessment of
1563 was reissued without alteration until at least 1589.[6]
In Wiltshire, the 1605 assessment was apparently reissued
for nearly thirty years, that of 1635 for nearly twenty, and
that of 1655 for another thirty.[7] In Ipswich, reissues are

[1] N.R.Q.S.R. VII, 128.
[2] Hertford C.R. VII, 3, 14, 26, 36, 48, 58, 68.
[3] Ibid. VI, 400.
[4] Ipswich Q.S. Records, Easter 1656.
[5] E.g. Suffolk Q.S. Order Books, April 1748; and Salop C.R. I, 109.
[6] E.H.R. XLI, 273.
[7] H.M.C. Various I, 161–75.

found for every year in the period 1618-46, and most of the years 1608-49.[1] In the West Riding, the 1647 assessment probably remained in force up to 1671.[2] In Shropshire, reissues are to be found for many of the years between 1653 and 1669;[3] reissues exist for all but two of the years between 1692 and 1712;[4] while the 1732 assessment was apparently issued without alteration up to 1739.[5] Reissues, with gaps, are to be found in the first half of the eighteenth century for Devonshire,[6] while the 1679 spinners' rates for that county were renewed without change up to 1790.[7] The Middlesex records show reissues for practically every year between 1610 and 1725;[8] while the Warwickshire assessment of 1738 held good, we are told, until 1773.[9]

What interpretation are we to place on all this reissuing of existing scales? One point at least is clear—that unless an unbroken series exists, care should be taken not to assume too much. Thus, despite the run of reissues for Middlesex just mentioned, a scholar who has worked through these records thinks (on the evidence of a court order requiring punishment for overpayment) that a new assessment was probably made about 1682;[10] even so, the absence of presentments for infringing the assessment between 1660 and 1760, in view of the Court's own statement in 1694 that there was widespread disregard of the assessed rates, suggests that reissue was, in that county and period, largely a matter of form.[11] Reissues have been held to be significant as showing at least a certain amount of administrative activity on the part of the justices.[12] Tawney would, how-

[1]Ipswich Q.S. Records.
[2]E.J. XXIV, 228.
[3]Salop C.R. I, 5, 14, 26, 56, 64, 88, 95, 98, 102, 106.
[4]Ibid. I, 140, 146, 151, 156, 162, 167, 180, 187, 193, 198, 205, 212, 219, 224, 229, 233, 236; II, 4, 8, 11.
[5]E.J. IV, 516.
[6]Gilboy, 88.
[7]Hoskins, 130.
[8]Dowdell, 149.
[9]Ashby, 176.
[10]Dowdell, 149-50.
[11]Ibid. 150.
[12]E.H.R. XLIII, 402.

ever, go further than this—"such orders are . . . evidence for the practice of assessment as complete as the issue of actual rates".[1] My own feeling is that the significance of a run of reissues cannot be judged in isolation, that it must be considered in conjunction with several other factors, of which lack of change in the cost-of-living or in the demand for labour, a certain relation between assessed and economic rates, and the known activity of justices and those acting on their instructions in publishing rates and presenting those infringing these rates are the most important. The presence of any one of these factors may be sufficient to convince me that reissue was more than a matter of form, as, for instance, when the Suffolk justices go to the expense of having the rates reprinted and distributed.[2] On the other hand, the absence of any corroborative evidence of one of these types strongly predisposes me to believe that the monotonous reissue of a thirty-year-old order does not mean the practice of assessment in any sense that matters.

Turning to the assessments themselves, the most noticeable feature about them is their astonishing variety in form and in types of work covered. Some are very lengthy, include piece-rates as well as time-rates, and go into detail on such matters as allowance for livery and for board and lodging. The Hull form used in the late seventeenth and early eighteenth centuries also details the charges of porters for carrying goods of varying types to different parts of the town.[3] Others are extremely short as, for instance, the Norwich assessment of 1657—"wages for men servants by the year £3, women servants 40s. and meat and drink, master workmen of carpenters, tilers, masons, reeders and the like to have 18d. a day and their labourer 12d. a day".[4] A tendency for assessments to become less detailed, which might be inferred from a comparison of Northamptonshire assessments for 1560 and 1667,[5] is not borne out by com-

[1] *V.S.W.* XI, 335.
[2] Suffolk Q.S. Order Books, April 1748.
[3] It would be of interest to know whether this was done in other ports.
[4] Norwich Q.S. Minutes, August 1657.
[5] *Econ. H.R.* I, 130.

parison of Kent assessments of 1563 and 1724,[1] of Hull
ratures of 1570 and 1721, or of Holland schedules of 1563
and 1680. Such an apparent tendency is sometimes to be
explained by the practice of merely mentioning those rates
which were to be altered, or by that of assessment by
divisions.[2] Indeed, the Act of 1603,[3] by removing any
ambiguity as to whether those outside husbandry and the
"enumerated occupations" were covered must, one would
think, have tended to make assessments more, rather than
less, detailed.[4] Assessments were, of course, modified to
meet changing needs and conditions, but the exact significance of these alterations cannot normally be grasped by
those without detailed local knowledge. Such changes of
form took place in Hertfordshire, for example, between
1631 and 1678 or 1687,[5] the 1631 form dating back to at
least 1592.[6] Differences between one town and another,
or one county and another, in the range of occupations
covered are presumably to be explained, inter alia, by the
relative strength of their trade associations. There is more
than a hint of this in the sentence appearing in the 1621
Faversham assessment—"Smithes, shoomakers, and other
trades worke by Rate wee knowe not"[7]—and in the New
Sarum declaration that it was best not to meddle with
rates for certain classes of work.[8] Outside the towns the
position was different, hence the statement in a Holland
rature for 1563—"the saide servaunties, and apprentyces
of Husbandry, Labourers, and Artificers hereafter named,
and al other Artyfycers not named, shall have and take the
several wages hereafter appoynted and not above".[9] There

[1]*E.H.R.* XLIII, 400.   [2]*E.H.R.* LII, 287.
[3]1 Jac. I.c.6.
[4]The repeal in 1757 of the Act of 1756 had, of course, a contrary
tendency; but few assessments survive after that date. Miss Hindmarsh found 17th century ratures more detailed than those of an earlier
date.
[5]*Hertford C.R.* I, 292: VI, 400.
[6]*Ibid.* I, 8–12.
[7]*Archaeologia Cantiana* XVI, 270.
[8]Hindmarsh, 160.
[9]A copy of this Proclamation is in the library at Queen's College,
Oxford.

were, of course, ample precedents for interference by the
Mayor and other town officers in the fixing of wages within
the different crafts, so that we sometimes find such interference still taking place, after 1563, quite independently
of the wage assessment provisions of 5 Elizabeth c. 4. In
Chester, for instance, it was in 1576 ordered by the "Maior,
Aldermen, Sheriffs, and Comen Counsaile, that the rate
price and weighte of spyninge, cardinge, wevinge, walkinge,
fullinge and dyinge of woll hereafter followinge shalbe
from hensfurthe observed and kept, viz., that no manner of
person or persons within this citie shall take or receyve for
spyninge and hande cardinge of one waight of woll above
sixe pens, . . . nor for weveinge any peece of wollen cloth
. . . contayninge xxii yards in length, above twelve
pens . . .".[1] Time-rates for work of some of the types mentioned in the Order had already been laid down in assessments under the Statute,[2] but not piece-rates.

The extent to which adjacent counties acted in concert
in their wage assessment policy is a matter of some interest.
A glance at the list of assessments in Appendix I suggests
that, on a number of occasions, the same factors must have
led to the rating of wages roughly simultaneously by
different groups of justices. This is probably why there are
several assessments in 1647 and the following year; the
justices of Lindsey, Kingston-upon-Hull and the East
Riding were presumably influenced by the same considerations in 1669; there is evidence that this was so in East and
North Yorkshire in 1679-80; and concerted action between
the justices of three adjacent counties is suggested by the
ratures of 1687 for Buckinghamshire, Hertfordshire and
Oxfordshire. We know that the East Riding justices sought
the advice of their fellow magistrates in the other two
Ridings on wage assessment on at least one occasion. An
East Riding Order of 1721 was to the effect "that such of
his Majesties Justices of the Peace for this Riding as shall
appear at the next Assizes held for the County of York be

---

[1]Morris, 409: *V.S.W.* XI, 317.
[2]*Ibid.* 367–8.

desired to meet any or such of his Majesties Justices of the
Peace as shall also appear for the other two Ridings in order
to settle servants and labourers wages that they make a
report thereof against the next Easter Sessions".[1]   On the
other hand, the known dates of reassessment in East Anglia
suggest that the different groups of justices involved acted
independently of each other in this matter, as will be seen
from the accompanying table.   Information regarding
assessed rates at the same date in adjacent areas tends to be
inconclusive, as there are so many doubts about the com-
parability of different categories of work.

EAST ANGLIAN ASSESSMENTS AND REISSUES
1631-1663
(Blanks normally indicate absence of records)

	Ipswich	Suffolk	Norwich	Norfolk
1631	Reissue		Reissue	
1632	Reissue		Reissue	
1633	Reissue		Reissue	
1634	Reissue		Assessment	
1635	Reissue		Reissue	
1636	Reissue		No mention	
1637	Reissue		Reissue	
1638	Reissue		Reissue	
1639	Reissue		Reissue	
1640	Reissue		Assessment	
1641	Reissue		Reissue	
1642	Reissue		Reissue	
1643	Reissue		Reissue	Reissue
1644	Reissue		Reissue	
1645	Reissue		Reissue	
1646	Reissue		Reissue	
1647	No mention		Reissue	
1648	Reissue		No mention	
1649	Reissue		Apparent Reissue	
1650	No mention	Reissue	Assessment	Reissue
1651		Reissue	No mention	Reissue

[1]East Riding Order Book, July 1721.

	Ipswich	Suffolk	Norwich	Norfolk
1652	Reissue	No mention	Reissue	Reissue
1653	Reissue	Reissue	Reissue	Reissue
1654	No further	Reissue	Reissue	Reissue
1655	mention	Reissue	Reissue	
1656		Assessment	Reissue	
1657		Reissue	Assessment	
1658		Reissue	Reissue	
1659		Reissue	No mention	
1660		Reissue	Reissue	
1661		Reissue	Reissue	Assessment
1662		Reissue	Reissue	Assessment
1663		Reissue	No further	Reissue
			mention	

Earlier writers have been led, by an examination of the dates of known assessments and reissues, to certain conclusions regarding periods of general activity in the rating of wages. Hewins, for example, suggested that activity was greatest in seven short periods (1563-7: 1591-6: 1608-12: 1619-21: 1632-4: 1651-5: and 1682-8), and that special reasons could be assigned for this.[1] Although this is clearly true up to a point (as will be shown in subsequent chapters), it is hardly a statement that would be made to-day. There are few periods of more than a year or two, until we reach the second half of the eighteenth century, for which evidence of activity in some part of the country is lacking. Even at the height of the Civil War the administrative work of Quarter Sessions was not everywhere suspended, while during the Commonwealth the Statute of Artificers was still regarded as a valuable piece of social legislation.[2] To attempt to go further than this, and calculate an annual or decennial "density" on the basis of known assessments and reissues would be, except for one or two groups of abnormal years, statistically valueless, however; for one thing, the years after 1670 or so would be unduly weighted by the

[1] E.J. VIII, 345.
[2] Lipson III, 260-1.

volume of sessions records which has survived and been printed for that period. Tawney, it is worth noticing, does not regard the evidence of the authors of legal textbooks as to the regularity of the practice of assessment as carrying much weight.[1] Only for particular localities—and then only with certain important reservations—are we justified, in my opinion, in making any general statements regarding periods of activity.

Finally, it may be said that a position has now been reached at which, so far as the practice of assessment in any particular area is concerned, the onus of proof rests on those who think the rating of wages was not practised. Cases in which there is no evidence of assessment at *any* date within a given Quarter Sessions area are becoming more and more rare. There is the case of Hertford, mentioned earlier in this chapter, but there lack of authority may have been the obstacle. Cases in which there is positive evidence that wages were never assessed are not, so far as I know, on record.[2]

---

[1] *V.S.W.* XI, 333.

[2] "Court's suggestion (*Rise of Midland Industries*, 59) that wage assessment was not practiced in Worcestershire, Warwickshire and Staffordshire in the 16th and 17th centuries is disproved by the data given in Appendix I."

CHAPTER II

THE EXTENT OF INFRINGEMENT

IT was one thing to draw up and publish a scale of maximum rates of wages (for, except in the cases to be discussed in chapter five, it was a question of maxima and not minima) but quite another to ensure that these rates would not be exceeded. The Statute, it is true, prescribed ten days' imprisonment and a fine of five pounds for giving higher wages, and twenty-one days' imprisonment for receiving higher wages;[1] while by fixing a copy of the scale on church doors, proclaiming it on certain market days, and instructing petty constables to acquaint every family with it[2] and high constables to make it known at their petty sessions, the authorities made sure that no one could justifiably plead ignorance. In other ways too, as will be shown later, entering into contracts of service which infringed the assessed rates was both difficult and attended with disadvantages. Nevertheless, if it was in the immediate interests of both parties to break the law, and when the agents of the law were overworked, practically unpaid, and perhaps even, on occasion, sympathetic, risks were likely to be taken. What evidence, then, do we possess regarding the effectiveness of the justices' scales? Direct evidence—which is all we shall be concerned with in the present chapter—is of two main types. On the one hand, there are the cases of infringement which were brought to the notice of the justices; while on the other hand, comparison can be made between wages known to have been paid and the

[1] 5 Eliz. c. 4, sec. 13.
[2] E.J. XXIV, 230.

15

corresponding assessed rates. As a matter of convenience, these two types of evidence may be considered separately.

Of what might be called specifically wage-assessment offences there were three (excluding the offence of not being present at the sessions for the rating of wages, which was an afterthought[1] and not often treated as an offence[2]). They were giving and accepting more than the assessed rates, and refusing to work for the assessed rates. To take the first of these, the bulk of our examples come from the North Riding of Yorkshire. Thus in January 1606-7 the inhabitants of a parish were collectively presented for giving excessive wages;[3] and four other cases were brought up at the same sessions.[4] There were three cases[5] between then and Easter Sessions 1608, when seven people were presented for this offence.[6] There were two further instances that year,[7] while at the sessions held in January 1608-9 four more presentments are recorded.[8] Except for three cases in 1610-11[9] (one of which is the only instance in the series we know to have concerned daily, as distinct from yearly, wages[10]), one in 1614[11] and one in 1647[12] there is then complete silence on the subject until, in the early sixteen-eighties, there is an outburst of overpayment associated, in my view, with a temporarily acute shortage of labour. This will be discussed at a later stage in the present study.[13] In Kesteven three cases (one concerned with daily wages[14]) are recorded in 1684,[15] and one instance

[1] 5 Eliz. c. 4. sec. 12 (Tawney and Power, I, 344).
[2] Cf. E.J. IV, 513.
[3] N.R.Q.S.R. I, 60.
[4] Ibid. I, 60.
[5] Ibid. I, 87, 105.
[6] Ibid. I, 111.
[7] Ibid. I, 122, 127.
[8] Ibid. I, 142-4.
[9] Ibid. I, 202, 207, 209.
[10] Ibid. I, 202.
[11] Ibid. II, 37.
[12] Ibid. IV, 270.
[13] Post, 93-100.
[14] Kesteven Q.S. Minutes, 216.
[15] Ibid. 216, 228.

two years earlier.[1] In Middlesex an instance occurred in 1564,[2] and in Hertfordshire there was one in 1655.[3] In Nottinghamshire we are told there were many presentments for giving and receiving more than the assessed rates in the seventeenth century —one of these was in 1606-7, and another in 1627.[4] In the latter part of the seventeenth century the Buckinghamshire justices observed that, as a result of failure to adapt assessed rates to the needs of the times[5] "both masters and servants had been and were subjected to indictments for their disobedience and contempts of the orders of the Court."[6] To this printed evidence there can be added a few cases which I have come across in the manuscript material examined—two Lindsey instances in 1655[7] and 1658,[8] and two for Suffolk, in 1564[9] and in the seventeen-twenties.[10] Miss Hindmarsh's survey of manuscript sessions records yielded thirty-six Essex cases of giving and receiving excessive wages in twenty-four years of the sixteenth century, masters usually being the offenders.[11] In addition, she mentions a Sussex instance of giving and taking more than the assessed rates in 1683, and four Hertfordshire examples of the same type for the period 1655-66.[12]

Cases of accepting more than the assessed rates are even less common. The North Riding Records (excluding the abnormal period of the early sixteen-eighties, already mentioned) only yield four cases (of which two appear to involve daily wages[13]) one in 1607-8,[14] one in 1609,[15] one in 1610,[16]

[1]Kesteven Q.S. Minutes, 138.
[2]Middlesex C.R. I, 50.
[3]Hertford C.R. I, 112.
[4]Copnall, 66.
[5]Actually wages had been reassessed ten years previously.
[6]Hewins, 86.
[7]Lindsey Q.S. Rolls, 1655.
[8]Ibid. 1658.
[9]Ipswich Q.S. Records, 1564.
[10]Book of Precedents and Indictments, 89.
[11]Hindmarsh, 129.
[12]Ibid. 284.
[13]N.R.Q.S.R. I, 171, 202.
[14]Ibid. I, 99.
[15]Ibid. I, 171.
[16]Ibid. I, 202.

and one in 1612.[1] There is one Kesteven case, in 1684,[2] and one Hertfordshire instance, in 1655,[3] while in 1632 in Wiltshire the tythingmen of Tinhead presented two sawyers, two carpenters and a thatcher "that doth exceed in taking of wages contrary to the Statute", but reported that they knew of no covenant servants committing the same offence.[4] A few instances can be added from manuscript records consulted, but not many. There is an interesting group of cases in the Thetford (Norfolk) Court Books, where, under the date 22nd April 1571, it is recorded that four men took wages contrary to the rate. Three of these appear to have been masons' labourers, and their offence was that of taking fourpence a day. The fourth (who, it may be guessed, had taken too great yearly wages) was punished in the stocks, instead of the statutory twenty-one days' imprisonment.[5] After a careful examination of loose sheets relating to Scarborough Courts of various kinds, four instances were found, two in 1627[6] and two others representing the presentment twice over of a certain Miles Cooper "for taking wages above the Statute about August last . . . and about 16 July last"—clearly not a yearly wage.[7] Finally, an instance of a bricklayer "taking and demanding" excessive wages is recorded for Holland in 1675;[8] and two Lindsey examples occurred in 1625 and 1655 respectively.[9] Miss Hindmarsh found cases, additional to the "mixed" types already mentioned, in Northamptonshire in the sixteen-sixties and eighties, (nine instances), in Hertfordshire in 1646 and 1650, and in Surrey in 1669.[10]

The relative scarcity of instances of these two offences is, therefore, plain. It is true that a recent writer, speaking

[1]N.R.Q.S.R. I, 266.
[2]Kesteven Q.S. Minutes, 228.
[3]Hertford C.R. I, 112.
[4]Wilts. C.R. 105-6.
[5]5 Eliz. c. 4, sec. 13.
[6]Scarborough Sessions Records, 9 April 1627.
[7]Ibid. 7 Jan. 1638-9.
[8]Holland Q.S. Minutes, Xmas 1675.
[9]Lindsey Q.S. Rolls.
[10]Hindmarsh, 284-5.

of these offences, observes "to this aspect the orders of sessions and presentments constantly refer",[1] but this view would seem to give undue weight to North Yorkshire experience. Other workers in this field have commented rather on their scarcity. Tawney, for instance, found no instances in the manuscript proceedings of Warwickshire Quarter Sessions for the period 1610-80,[2] Heaton comments on the paucity of cases in the West Riding,[3] Cunningham's general impression was that steps were not taken.[4] Turning to the explanation of this scarcity the commonest view is, as one would expect, that it constitutes proof that these sections of the Statute were not enforced.[5] In the case of Buckinghamshire, one writer observes "the laws against masters who gave more than the legal wage were . . . not enforced; there are no presentments of such offences, and the bench of magistrates even ordered a master to pay his servant wages that . . . exceeded the maximum".[6] Chambers suggests that the more powerful masters (e.g. the Duke of Rutland) could safely ignore the Statute "as their social prestige would reduce, if not eliminate, the risk of prosecution at Quarter Sessions".[7] Heaton, on the other hand, does not agree that an absence of cases indicates failure to apply the Act. "By its very nature and by its threats of penalties, the Act was an easy one to obey".[8] Hewins, on the strength of Buckinghamshire evidence of "unjustified" indictments mentioned earlier, reaches the same conclusion from the other side—the laxity of the justices is not necessarily disproved even if numerous cases of overpayment occur in the records.[9] My own view is that we are not justified in inferring from the lack of such cases that the justices' scales had no effect unless *for the same area and date*

[1]*Kesteven Q.S. Minutes*, p. cxi.
[2]*V.S.W.* XI, 563.
[3]*E.J.* XXIV, 231.
[4]*Ibid.* IV, 513.
[5]*Ibid.* IV, 513.
[6]*V.C.H. Bucks.* II, 71.
[7]Chambers, 279.
[8]*E.J.* XXIV, 231.
[9]Hewins, 86.

it can be shown that actual wages in excess of these scales were being paid. Before proceeding to examine this aspect of the matter, however, the third type of wage assessment offence may be dealt with.

It could no doubt be objected that "refusal to serve for the assessed rates" was not, under the Statute of Artificers, distinguishable as an offence from mere "refusal to serve". It is, of course, true that there were a number of circumstances in which a person could be compelled to serve, and that no particular stipulation regarding the rate of wages at which this service should be undertaken was made. Thus those who had been brought up in one of the "enumerated occupations",[1] or had been attached to it for three years, and were unmarried, (or, if married, under thirty), who failed to fulfil a minimum property condition, and were not legally retained elsewhere, could be compelled to serve in that occupation at the request of any master.[2] Again, every person between twelve and threescore years, not being already lawfully retained or apprenticed and not having a minimum property qualification, could be compelled to serve in husbandry by the year.[3] Unmarried women between the ages of twelve and forty could, at the discretion of two justices, be compelled to serve by the year or week or day for such wages as were thought fit.[4] At harvest time artificers and persons fit to labour could be compelled to serve *by the day*.[5] Only in one of these cases, it will be noticed, is anything said about wages, and on that occasion what is said is vague enough. The offence "refusing to work for the assessed rates" was, however, made perfectly clear in two later Statutes. Thus in 1572[6] and 1597[7] "all common Labourers being persons able in Bodye using loytering, and refusinge to worke for suche reasonable

[1] 5 Eliz. c. 4, sec. 2.
[2] 5 Eliz. c. 4, sec. 3.
[3] 5 Eliz. c. 4, sec. 5.
[4] 5 Eliz. c. 4, sec. 17.
[5] 5 Eliz. c. 4, sec. 15.
[6] 14 Eliz. c. 5.
[7] 39 Eliz. c. 4.

Wages as ys taxed and comonly gyven in suche partes"[1] were declared to be vagabonds, and were to be treated as such. This being so the phrase "refusing to work", where met with in presentments and indictments, is very often accompanied by mention of the justices' rates. For many purposes it would, of course, be sufficient to class several varieties of refusal to work together—living idly, living at one's own hands, refusing to work for the assessed wages. But for this study cases where it is definitely stated that the refusal was of this latter character are of special interest, however much we may regret our inability to determine what proportion of the residue should really be included in this category. For, where this particular aspect of the offence is stressed the refusal, one may infer, amounted to a demand for higher wages than those in the justices' scale— a demand, at least, of a somewhat more direct character than "living idly" which, however often it may have been an indication of precisely the same maladjustment,[2] must sometimes have had a simpler explanation.[3]

As before, the North Riding and Kesteven provide the bulk of our examples. In North Yorkshire there were five instances in October 1610. Three men were presented "for denying to worke emongest their neighbours in Harvest, and for departing forth of the Libertie for greater wages";[4] while at a special sessions held later in the same month a man was presented for refusing to thatch "for such wages as is allowed", and another for refusing to thresh under fourpence a day, though this last entry is crossed out.[5] In 1614 a rough-waller was presented for, *inter alia*, refusing to work for statute wages, and going forth of the Riding "into other cuntryes to worke in sommer so as his neighboures cannot have his worke in hay-time and harvest".[6]

---

[1] 14 Eliz. c. 5, sec. 5.
[2] *I.e* between assessed and economic rates of wages.
[3] The other offences mentioned in this paragraph will be considered in chapter three.
[4] *N.R.Q.S.R.* I, 202.
[5] *Ibid.* I, 220.
[6] *Ibid.* II, 53.

3

Three instances are to be found in the Kesteven Minutes for the sixteen-seventies—one in 1675[1] and two in 1678.[2] There are one or two early Middlesex examples in the fifteen-sixties;[3] while the Oxfordshire justices decided in 1694 that if a certain William Wakelin of Whately did not work "at such rates as the town shall allow", the next justice should send him to the House of Correction.[4] Finally, so far as the printed materials go, the West Riding justices in 1641, acting on "the generall complainte of the inhabitants of these partes, that servants refuse to worke for reasonable wages, and cannot be hired for competent allowance as formerlye, makeing advantage of the much busines of the times" ordered that the Statute should be observed;[5] while, on the other hand, the justices of a Derbyshire wapentake reported, ten years earlier, that none were presented to them for living out of service and refusing to work for reasonable wages.[6] Two Holland cases were noted in the manuscript materials examined, one in 1673[7] and one in 1678.[8] Such, meagre as it is, is the evidence available on refusing to work for the assessed rates.

Turning now to the comparison of assessed with *actual* rates it will be remembered that Hewins took Thorold Rogers to task for comparing averages deficient in northern wages with northern assessments and concluding that the market rates were higher than assessed rates.[9] Hewins's own view was that the justices' scales could be accepted as representing current wages in the various counties at the time they were promulgated.[10] Almost inevitably, everyone whose researches have brought him into contact with assessments has associated himself with one or other of these

[1]*Kesteven Q.S. Minutes*, 35.
[2]*Ibid.* 86, 93.
[3]*Middlesex C.R.* I, 63.
[4]Gretton, p. lxxix.
[5]*W.R.S. Records 1611–42*, 333.
[6]*V.C.H. Derby* II, 182: Bland, 389.
[7]Holland Q.S. Minutes, Mich. 1673.
[8]*Ibid.* Xmas 1678.
[9]Hewins, 83.
[10]*Ibid.* 87.

views. No study of the rating of wages would be complete, therefore, without some mention of this controversial topic; so that, unsatisfactory as the evidence is in most respects, some attempt must be made to review it here. In the North Riding, daily rates paid to thatchers in 1681 and masons and carpenters in 1687 and 1691 in Topcliffe[1] were in accordance with the justices' scale of 1658[2] (a new assessment was, it is true, drawn up in 1680,[3] but it is unlikely—as will appear in the discussion[4] of the circumstances making that assessment necessary—that daily rates were altered). Scarborough masons in 1657 and carpenters in 1667 were found[5] to be receiving slightly higher rates but this was, of course, a normal feature of town economy, and wages there were in any case separately assessed. In the West Riding, we are told that "the average daily earnings of the weaver in the seventeenth century were . . . well below the maximum[6] fixed by the assessment of 1647";[7] and that up to about 1730 the wage lists were being enforced, but not thereafter.[8] It would appear from wages recorded in a private account book relating to Penistone,[9] however, that there were divergencies between assessed and economic rates earlier than that. Thus a carpenter was paid 1s. 2d. a day in 1694, though 12d. was the maximum a master carpenter who took charge of a building and had two or three under him was allowed to take; while numbers of men mowing and women haymaking were overpaid in 1693.[10] A joiner at Masham appears to have been overpaid in 1669.[11] In the East Riding, the wages given in an Everingham account book[12] are in accordance with

[1]Topcliffe Churchwardens' Accounts.
[2]*N.R.Q.S.R.* VI, 3–4.
[3]*Ibid.* VII, 45.
[4]*Post*, 93–100.
[5]Scarborough Corporation Miscellaneous Accounts.
[6]In the West Riding even the rates for clothworkers were maxima.
[7]Heaton, 115: *E.J.* XXIV, 234.
[8]*E.J.* XXIV, 232.
[9]Captain Bosseville's Account Book.
[10]The 1691 husbandry wages were, however, correct.
[11]Masham Churchwardens' Accounts.
[12]Philip Constable's Account Book.

the rature of 1669.[1] Those in a Welwick farmer's accounts,[2] given under the heading "servants and their wages" are not so in all cases, however. Thus, although we have no knowledge of the assessed rates current in the years 1659-67, if the 1669 rature is any guide to them two maidservants must have been overpaid in 1659 and 1660; and the same would be true of some women harvesting in 1666 and a thatcher in the previous year. Moreover four maidservants were definitely overpaid in 1673 and the four following years, by comparison with the highest rates given in the 1669 assessment, as were two men who were paid higher wages in 1674 and 1675 than that applicable to a bailiff of husbandry; though the majority of the wages recorded were below the appropriate maxima.

Turning to Lancashire, a comparison of the 1725 assessment and the wages given by Arthur Young in 1768 shows remarkably little difference between the two.[3] In Derbyshire there are indications that mid-seventeenth century payments to day labourers in husbandry were in accordance with the 1634 rature; and that masons and their labourers in 1693 were receiving the amounts given in the 1648 assessment.[4] Rutland yearly wages recorded at statute sessions between 1626 and 1634 are said to have been in accordance with the rature of 1610;[5] it is, of course, unlikely that failure to comply with the assessed rates would be officially recorded by the master breaking the law. For the same reason, our knowledge that the wage agreements recorded in the Norwich Court Books did not infringe the official scale is not, perhaps, of very great value. In Warwickshire (where the 1738 rature was reissued until 1773) there is evidence that unemployed labourers were, in 1770, receiving allowances supplementing their wages which brought their earnings above the justices' rates, and

---

[1]*E.H.R.* LII, 284-6.
[2]Welwick Byelawmen's and Miscellaneous Accounts Book.
[3]Gilboy, 174-5.
[4]*V.C.H. Derby* II, 182-3.
[5]Rogers, *History* VI, 693.

in 1778 the justices overpaid a thatcher;[1] in the latter case, however, we do not know that the 1738 scale was even officially recognized. Two bills of repairs for work done on Magdalene Bridge in 1688-9[2] include some wages which appear to be in excess of those allowed by the 1687 assess-ment[3] for Oxfordshire; Mrs. Gilboy, too, found large dis-crepancies between masons' and carpenters' actual wages and those given in the rature of 1701,[4] but her *agricultural* information is for too late a period to enable any inference to be drawn in that case.[5] The Buckinghamshire position is very similar to that of Oxfordshire. Here, too, wages were reassessed in 1687, and market rates seem to have been out of alignment with this scale. The justices them-selves ordered a master to pay his servant a wage at a yearly rate exceeding the maximum allowed, while we are told that "the regular rate for ordinary labour seems already to have been 1s. a day with but little variation, though the legal amount was 8d. at most; but in the more skilled work the difference as usual was even greater. Instead of 1s. 2d. a bricklayer was entered as receiving 2s., a carpenter 1s. 6d., and a plumber, whose trade did not appear in the scale of wages, had 2s. 6d. a day".[6] Nor did the increases in yearly rates sanctioned in the 1765 rature anything like keep pace with the increases in amounts actually paid to workers on a comparable basis.[7] Turning to Hertfordshire, it appears from various accounts for work done for the county town that the assessed rates were exceeded. Thus in July 1629 a mason was paid 9d. for half a day's work, the summer rate for artificers of the best sort in the 1631 rature being only 1s. 4d. a day; a carpenter was, however, paid at the correct rate on the same occasion. In April 1633 a carpenter was paid at the rate of 1s. 6d. a day; and artificers (either carpenters or masons) were

[1]Ashby, 176.
[2]Gretton, 69, 94.
[3]*Ibid*. pp. lxii-lxiv.
[4]Gilboy, 110.
[5]*Ibid*. 89.
[6]*V.C.H Bucks*. II, 71.
[7]*Ibid*. II, 84.

26 WAGE REGULATION UNDER THE STATUTE OF ARTIFICERS

getting 1s. 6d. and 1s. 8d. in 1635 and 1636 (two instances
of 1s. 6d. a day occur in the winter of 1636, the official
winter maximum being 1s.), a carpenter in July 1637 getting 1s. 9d. a day.[1] It may, of course, be objected that rates
in the town would naturally be somewhat higher than those
in the surrounding district. One writer finds still greater
discrepancies between assessed and actual rates in Hertfordshire.[2] His case is based, however, on a comparison of a
labourer's 1s. a day in a 1659 account[3] and 10d. and 1s. a
day for work on the highways in 1672[4] on the one hand,
and the winter rate for general labour—4d. or 5d. a day—in
the St. Albans liberty assessment of 1631.[5] Quite apart
from the obvious dangers of comparing rates separated by
such long periods of time, the assessed rate that should have
been chosen for comparison is certainly that *without* meat
and drink—10d. in the 1631 assessment. Wages given to
carpenters in a 1683 bill[6] fall within the limits laid down in
the 1678 rature.[7] Wages mentioned by yearly servants in
three petitions alleging non-payment, one in 1635-6,[8] one
in the latter half of the century,[9] and one in 1732,[10] accord
with the assessed rates then current. An eight-pound-a-
year wage mentioned in a 1680 petition,[11] however, exceeds
by three pounds the highest wage given in the 1678 assessment.[12] Comparison of bricklayers' and carpenters' bills for
county work with the 1724 Kent rature shows the actual
rates to be considerably higher than those assessed,[13] and
the position with regard to the Gloucestershire assessment

[1] All these rates are taken from miscellaneous accounts for the town
of Hertford.
[2] *V.C.H. Herts.* IV, 228.
[3] *Hertford C.R.* I, 130.
[4] *Ibid.* I, 233.
[5] Clutterbuck I, pp. xxii–xxiv.
[6] *Hertford C.R.* I, 339.
[7] *Ibid.* I, 292.
[8] *Ibid.* V, 209.
[9] *Ibid.* I, 207.
[10] *Ibid.* VII, 238.
[11] *Ibid.* VI, 332.
[12] *Ibid.* I, 292.
[13] *E.H.R.* XLIII, 404.

of 1732 is similar.[1] This, as Mrs. Gilboy points out, is particularly significant, since the bills concerned had to be examined by a committee of justices.[2] A comparison between the daily agricultural rates assessed for Gloucestershire in 1732 and Arthur Young's figures for 1768 does not, however, show any marked disparity.[3] Roughly the same position is found in eighteenth-century Devonshire—higher rates than those rated in the building trades,[4] particularly in the towns, but no very noticeable discrepancy in daily rates in husbandry.[5]

What conclusions can we draw from the evidence examined? In the first place, there is clearly a tendency for assessed and actual rates to diverge in the eighteenth century. Secondly, this tendency is, on the whole, most marked in the building trades and least marked in daily rates for work in husbandry. Thirdly, there is some doubt as to whether the assessed rates for the *county* ever had much relevance to *town* conditions; where towns rated their own wages, of course, this particular difficulty did not arise. Fourthly, the case for a divergence between assessed and economic rates before, say, the sixteen-eighties is still not proven; such material as is readily available suggests conformity between the two in that period, but a fuller examination of unpublished early farm account books and churchwardens' accounts might, in some districts, disprove this. Miss Hindmarsh, after working on manuscript materials different from those used in this study, came to the conclusion that, up to the middle of the seventeenth century, market and assessed rates corresponded fairly closely;[6] but that in the second half of the century there was a definite failure to restrain market rates for skilled labour (except in husbandry) from exceeding the assessed rates.[7]

[1]Gilboy, 110.
[2]*E.H.R.* XLIII, 404.
[3]Gilboy, 87.
[4]*Ibid.* 110–1.
[5]*Ibid.* 88–9.
[6]Hindmarsh, 105–6.
[7]*Ibid.* 301.

This failure she attributes not to magisterial laxity (though she admits the scarcity of recorded proceedings against those infringing the official scales)[1] but to the growth of a tendency to combination amongst journeymen and small masters which marked the break-up of the older types of guild, and other well-known tendencies accompanying these developments.[2] With the general outlines of this picture one could hardly quarrel, though it is perhaps a little more clear-cut than the uncertain and rather contradictory nature of the evidence justifies.

[1]Hindmarsh, 282.
[2]*Ibid.* 332–51.

CHAPTER III

COMPLEMENTARY PARTS OF THE POLICY: I

A S we have seen, several sections of the Statute of
Artificers made it an offence for people fulfilling
certain conditions to refuse to work under given circumstances. There was an additional deterrent to living idly,
in that a Statute of 1572 laid it down that "all and everye
persone . . . able to labour, haveinge nor Land or Maister,
nor using any lawfull Marchaundze Crafte or Mysterye
whereby hee or shee might get his or her Lyvinge" and
with no legal means of support was to be treated as a
vagabond.[1] There were, indeed, under these and other
statutes, ample means provided for taking proceedings
against masterless men and women, boys and girls, in the
parishes in which they were settled, and the justices were
not slow to avail themselves of them. The apprenticing of
poor children and the provision of a parish stock for setting
the poor on work—expedients which there is no need to
discuss here—represented, in fact, only part of a policy
of which the compelling of everyone who could legally be
forced to do so to obtain a service, or go to one found for
them, was another important element. The printed records
of sessions provide numerous examples of the latter (other
than those given in the previous chapter) and would, no
doubt, yield still more but for the fact that a single justice
had authority to order the idle able-bodied to work.[2] In
the North Riding, it is true, instances are rare. A mother
was presented in 1610 for keeping her son at home idly,[3]

[1] 14 Eliz. c. 5, sec. 5.
[2] Gretton, p. x.
[3] *N.R.Q.S.R.* I, 220.

and there is a case of refusal to serve in 1619;[1] but, except
for two women being presented in 1670,[2] there is no further
mention of the matter until the temporary labour shortage
of 1680-2, when the justices employed all the means at their
command, and naturally found their powers of compelling
to go to service of value in this emergency.[3] The Kesteven
minutes provide an instance, in 1692, of someone for whom
the overseers have found a service being threatened, in
case of refusal, with the House of Correction, "there to
remayne till she doe goe".[4] At a Shropshire Sessions held
three years earlier two women were given three months to
provide themselves with services, with the alternative of
the "House".[5] Two Surrey cases, in 1662-3, both concern
women.[6] A particularly determined effort was apparently
made by the Middlesex authorities in 1639, when no fewer
than twenty-two men were presented for being loose, idle
fellows living out of service under pretence of coal heaving
once or twice a month;[7] one later case is recorded, in
1665,[8] and quite a number of earlier ones, in the fifteen-
seventies and eighties.[9] In Buckinghamshire instances
occur in the sixteen-eighties at the rate of about one or two
a year; altogether between 1679 and 1690 eighteen cases
are recorded, of which five relate to women.[10] The justices
of a Derbyshire wapentake, as we noticed before, reported
in 1631 that there had been no presentments of this type;[11]
but the Wiltshire magistrates, as we shall see later, provided
a valuable clue—if one were needed—to the significance of
"living idly" in many cases, when in 1655 they made an

[1]*N.R.Q.S.R.* II, 213.
[2]*Ibid.* VI, 147.
[3]*Post,* 93–100.
[4]*Kesteven Q.S. Minutes,* 417.
[5]*Salop C.R.* I, 119.
[6]*Surrey Record Society* XIV, 150, 304.
[7]*Middlesex C.R.* III, 169–70.
[8]*Ibid.* III, 372–3.
[9]*Ibid.* I, 80, 131. A Chester case of about this date is given in
Morris, 358.
[10]*Bucks Sessions Records* I, 36, 74, 168, 177, 193, 234, 310, 319, 322,
328.
[11]Bland, 389.

order that no young men or maids fit to go to service (their parents not being of ability to keep them) should remain at home.[1] The Devonshire justices, in 1657, ordered all masterless persons to take masters within a month.[2]

The manuscript records examined throw additional light on the use of the justices' power in this matter.[3] In the first place, they suggest that during the sixteen-thirties and forties special efforts were made to compel people to obtain services. The justices of Thetford (Norfolk), for instance, ordered in 1634 that all persons inhabiting the borough who were compellable to serve in husbandry yet lived at their own hands should be apprehended by warrant and sent to the workhouse, until they were lawfully retained in husbandry for a year at least.[4] On the first of May the following year they issued a further order that all fit to go to service should provide themselves with one before the first of June next, on pain of the workhouse.[5] The justices of Hertford were kept busy dealing with parents who kept great girls at home idly, and with lusty young fellows able to do good service who yet preferred to live idly about the town. If the parent promised to take the necessary steps, further proceedings were usually dropped—at a Month's Court held in April 1628, for example, "Widow Watts did in open Court promise that her daughter be put out to service by Whit Sunday next."[6] All parents were not equally repentant, however, some being rash enough to voice their indignation at the interference of the law in the hearing of the local constable or ill-disposed neighbours— Robert Simmonds, presented in 1636 for keeping two girls at home that were fit for service, was heard to boast that Mister Mayor would place none of his.[7] Altogether, in the

---

[1]*H.M.C. Various* I, 132: Bland, 360.
[2]Hamilton, 164.
[3]Devreux Edgar's Diary shows a magistrate frequently acting in this matter on the complaint of individual inhabitants, the parish constable, or the churchwardens and overseers.
[4]Thetford Court Records, August 1634.
[5]*Ibid.* May 1635.
[6]Hertford Court Records, April 1628.
[7]*Ibid.* Sept. 1636.

Hertford records that survive for the years 1627 to 1641, fifty-seven cases (excluding where possible cases of "not apprenticing", though the similarity of the offence and the loose use made of such terms as "service" makes certainty impossible) are recorded, of which thirty-eight concern parents, and the remainder the people themselves. Sometimes there are as many as seven or eight instances brought up at one sessions, the peak years being 1629-30 and 1638-39. There are two cases additional to those mentioned, one in 1642 and one in 1645. Instances of roughly the same date are to be found in Norfolk[1] and Suffolk.[2]

Secondly, as one would expect, the normal punishment threatened or applied was the House of Correction. Norwich had, it is true, a good deal of trouble in 1624-5 with feltmakers who lived at their own hands, and threats of severer punishment were used, but these people had no settlement there, and the object was to make them leave the city.[3] Thirdly, there was, of course, lack of uniformity in such matters as the time allowed for providing oneself with a service—it varied, in the records examined, from three months or so[4] to no time at all,[5] a fortnight being quite a usual period;[6] one father obtained the discharge of his daughter from Bridewell on promising that she should be retained in service within a week.[7] In other respects, too, discretion had to be exercised by the justices. The exceptional circumstances which might justify a relaxation of the law in this matter are well illustrated by cases in the Suffolk Order Books. Thus two children who had been presented for going at their own hands were discharged from their indictments on it appearing that they were not fit to go to service "they being impotent and having scaldheads."[8]

[1]*E.g.* Norwich Court Records, July 1630.
[2]*E.g.* Suffolk Order Books, October 1642.
[3]Norwich Court Records.
[4]*Salop C.R.* I, 119.
[5]Suffolk Order Books, Jan. 1647–8.
[6]Norwich Court Records, Oct. 1659: Thetford Court Records, Oct. 1751.
[7]Norwich Court Records, Aug. 1623.
[8]Suffolk Order Books, Trinity 1659. This case, from other informa-

Another Suffolk case is worth giving in some detail. The inhabitants of a parish complained that a certain Elizabeth Nunn was fit to go to service notwithstanding the loss of one of her hands, but that she refused to serve anyone as a hired servant by the year. The Court thereupon ordered the inhabitants to provide her with a fitting service before next sessions, but one "that shall be approved and allowed by this Court". If she refused to accept this service, she should be sent to Bridewell.[1] At a later sessions it was reported that she had been duly offered a service with a master of whom the Court approved, but that "she refused to accept of him, and further said she would not accept any service but as she would provide for herself". The Court, however, taking into account the fact that she agreed to take this master on the Monday following the Saturday of her refusal (by which time he had obtained another servant), decided to extend the time-limit by another six months.[2] Here those most anxious to put the law in motion seem to have been the villagers, while the justices took a more lenient view of the case. On other occasions the magistrates, when their attention was drawn to disregard of the law, took special steps to enforce it. Thus at Norwich, on being informed by those concerned in the government of the trade of worsted weavers "that it is a general practice for young boys and lads under the age of twenty-one years to take work from worsterers by the gross, and so will take and leave work at their pleasure, which this Court looks upon to be the same thing as if they did live at their own hands and without any legal retainer", instructions were issued to churchwardens and overseers to give an exact account every month of all such persons.[3]

Finally, there is additional evidence both in the Ipswich and Suffolk records in the seventeen-twenties, that the assessment of wages and the enforcement of the laws

tion given, apparently concerned apprenticeship: the criteria applied would, however, be very similar.

[1] Suffolk Order Books, Hilary 1659.
[2] *Ibid.* Easter 1660.
[3] Norwich Court Records, Aug. 1668.

against living idly were, on occasion, very closely inter-related. Consideration of this aspect of the matter can, however, conveniently be postponed until a later stage.

Leaving the question of living out of service for the moment, we can go on to consider a group of offences of a rather similar type. Departing before the end of one's term, or leaving one's work unfinished was, after all, only a stage removed from living idly and refusing to go to service. The yearly contract of service which was compulsory in many occupations could only be broken by mutual consent and reasonable and sufficient cause shown to a justice,[1] and the servant wanting to depart in normal circumstances had to give one quarter's warning before the end of his term. The penalty for unlawful departure before term was imprisonment,[2] and provision was made for apprehending servants who fled to other counties.[3] Similarly, artificers and labourers leaving the work they had undertaken to do before it was finished were to be imprisoned for one month without bail and to forfeit five pounds to the aggrieved party;[4] when this latter penalty, incidentally, was inflicted on an East Riding carpenter he was also required to pay those that set him on work "such costs and damages as they shall be put unto in recovery thereof".[5] Instances of leaving before term are, as one might expect, to be found scattered throughout the North Riding records. Between 1605 and 1610 fourteen cases are recorded,[6] of which four were brought forward at one sessions in October 1608.[7] Thereafter instances are rarer—one in 1637[8] (when the offender was, the statutory penalty notwithstanding, fined ten shillings), one in 1642,[9] another

---

[1] 5 Eliz. c. 4, sec. 4. The justice's "allowing" was essential.
[2] 5 Eliz. c. 4, sec. 6.
[3] 5 Eliz. c. 4, sec. 39.
[4] 5 Eliz. c. 4, sec. 10.
[5] East Riding Q.S. Books, July 1649.
[6] N.R.Q.S.R. I, 11, 60, 68, 99, 131, 151, 156, 180, 202.
[7] Ibid. I, 131.
[8] Ibid. IV, 75.
[9] Ibid. IV, 232.

in 1655-6,[1] and another in 1662.[2] A milner failed to appear at all after being hired in 1663,[3] a carpenter a year or two later did not stay and finish laying a barn floor,[4] while an employer accused of not paying his servant the wages due to him made the counter-accusation that the servant had left before his term.[5] Heaton, after a search of half-a-dozen West Riding indictment books, only found one case of this character, in 1648,[6] and none are to be found in the published West Yorkshire records; a colliery workman was, however, committed to Bridewell in 1681 for breaking his contract of service.[7] There are two East Riding instances in 1648.[8] The number of pages referred to in the index to the Kesteven minutes under "work, refusing to perform" is deceptive, for thirteen of these prove to be concerned with only one instance. Actually there are only seven persons indicted, two in 1680[9] and five in 1683;[10] the offence is given in all cases as that of refusing to perform work undertaken. Lancashire provides a larger number of examples. Thus in 1600-1,[11] 1603[12] and 1605[13] there are orders that the servants named shall serve out their term, the servant involved in the last order being required to accept a subsequent service at three-fourths of her salary; while in the published records of certain Manchester sessions eighteen cases occur in the period 1616-22.[14] Nottinghamshire[15] and Worcestershire[16] provide one or two early seventeenth-century instances, the former involving

[1]*N.R.Q.S.R.* V, 206.
[2]*Ibid.* VI, 59.
[3]*Ibid.* VI, 75.
[4]*Ibid.* VI, 97.
[5]*Ibid.* VI, 174.
[6]*E.J.* XXIV, 231.
[7]W.R.S. Order Books, April 1681.
[8]East Riding Q.S. Books, April, July.
[9]*Kesteven Q.S. Minutes,* 119.
[10]*Ibid.* 158, 162.
[11]*Lancs. Q.S. Records* I, 83.
[12]*Ibid.* I, 192.
[13]*Ibid.* I, 272.
[14]*Manchester Sessions,* 3, 22, etc.
[15]Copnall, 68.
[16]*Worcs. C.R.* 215, 273.

masons failing to finish their work. Hertfordshire examples are few—three in the seventeenth[1] and three in the eighteenth century,[2] the latest being 1784[3]—but Middlesex provides even fewer (four, in 1565,[4] 1628,[5] 1686[6] and 1709-10[7]).

Other manuscript evidence does not suggest that this offence was common—or, more correctly, that it often formed the subject of Quarter Sessions presentments, indictments and orders. There are four Holland[8] and two Lindsey[9] cases in the sixteen-seventies, and one or two in the Norwich[10] and Suffolk[11] sessions records. There may, however, have been a good deal of activity, of which we know nothing, by justices acting out of sessions. From a Suffolk justice's diary it would appear that the issuing of warrants in connection with the unlawful departure of servants was of fairly common occurrence—in the six years 1703 to 1708 this particular magistrate issued forty-six warrants in connection with failure to finish work, leaving before term, or not entering service after being hired.[12] As to what, in addition, to such exceptional events as the death of one's master, tended to be regarded as reasonable and sufficient cause for not remaining the full term, it appears that the Suffolk justices, at least, were prepared to consider insufficient food and failure to pay wages as, on occasion, providing adequate justification. A servant who left her master because she did not get enough to eat was sent to her last place of lawful settlement, instead of being punished and sent back to her master, the Court being of opinion that

[1]*Hertford C.R.* V, 407: I, 112: VI, 346.
[2]*Ibid.* VII, 207: VIII 96, 329.
[3]*Ibid.* VIII, 329.
[4]*Middlesex C.R.* I, 54.
[5]*Ibid.* III, 21.
[6]Dowdell, 147.
[7]*Ibid.* 147.
[8]Holland Q.S. Minutes, 1674, 76, 77, 78 (also one or two later cases, *e.g.* 1682, 1684 and 1688).
[9]Lindsey Q.S. Minutes, 1675, 76 (also one earlier case, 1667).
[10]*E.g.* Norwich Court Records, Nov. 1615.
[11]*E.g.* Suffolk Order Books, June 1642: Jan. 1642-3.
[12]Devreux Edgar's Diary.

he was "in no wise fit to keep a servant, by reason of disability in estate".[1] Another servant was discharged of her service on it appearing that her master had detained her wages.[2] In one rather unusual Suffolk case a master complained that his servant had run away, but on examination of the servant it appeared that his master (who was a Dissenter) had tried to prevail on his servant by entreaty and threats to go to Dissenters' Meetings, and had found him work to do on Sundays in order to prevent his going to church. The master, on being threatened with further action if he did not humble himself, agreed to the discharge of his servant "by mutual consent".[3] Incidentally, it is perhaps worth noticing that the form of "imprisonment" quite usually[4] employed for leaving one's work was a period in the House of Correction—was this because those who had run away from their masters could conveniently be classed as idle or disorderly persons for whom, under the Statute of 1609-10,[5] Bridewells were to be provided, or did it mark the transition of these Houses from workhouses to prisons?[6] It is clear, at least, that the justices were acting on instructions in sending "dissolute or idle servants" to Bridewell.[7]

For the efficient working of the Elizabethan labour code it was, of course, essential that leaving one's work should be treated as an offence. For one thing, the enforcement of yearly hiring in many occupations would have lost much of its value if masters and servants were allowed to break contracts of service with impunity. For another thing, people not in regular employment were an evil example to those who had a taste for living idly, either at home or

[1]Suffolk Order Books, Easter 1659.
[2]*Ibid.* Easter 1660. The circumstances of the case *N.R.Q.S.R.* VII, 237, are not altogether clear.
[3]Devreux Edgar's Diary, November 1702.
[4]*E.g. N.R.Q.S.R.* VI, 59: *Hertford C.R.* VI, 346: Suffolk Order Books, June 1642: Norwich Court Records, Nov. 1615.
[5]7 Jac. I, c. 4. This is implied in a case mentioned in *V.C.H. Lincs.* II, 339.
[6]*Cf.* Gretton, p. lxxvii.
[7]*Manchester Sessions*, 58.

wandering abroad, and were likely, in the eyes of the authorities, to fall into evil ways. Again, departing at will led to all kinds of settlement difficulties. From the point of view of wage assessment in a narrow sense, however, one would be tempted to treat the prevalence of the offence in any locality at any time as evidence—if independent corroboration were possible—of a labour shortage. Yet in the records examined the volume of these cases is hardly at any point sufficient to suggest anything of this sort. It is of interest, therefore, to supplement these cases by examples of what is, in effect, the same offence committed by masters instead of servants. It will be remembered that the Statute required that servants in husbandry and the "enumerated occupations" should, on their lawful departure from the parish of their employment, obtain a testimonial[1] sealed by the constable and two householders certifying that their departure was in order;[2] and provided the penalty of being whipped and used as a vagabond for servants unable to produce such a testimonial within twenty-one days, and the penalty of a five-pound fine for masters retaining servants without requiring them to show their testimonials.[3] Instances of servants being indicted for not having testimonials are rare,[4] probably because they were normally proceeded against under the "unlawful departure" section, or because the particular form of their vagabondage was not given in the indictment (still less in the summary of the indictment in the sessions minutes). That proceedings were taken against masters hiring servants without testimonials

[1]The form of words commonly used in these testimonials is also given in Hampson, 274. They cost twopence; "some masters will give them that 2d. againe" (Farming Books of Henry Best, 134).
[2]5 Eliz. c. 4, sec. 7.
[3]5 Eliz. c. 4, sec. 8.
[4]At Norwich, however, a number were sent to Bridewell or "committed and punished"—e.g. Norwich Court Records, Nov. 1615: Aug. 1625: Mar. 1631: Apr. 1631. In a case in N.R.Q.S.R. I, 34, a servant so offending is merely sent back to her former service. A later memorandum is perhaps significant—"that there are presented . . . diverse servantes who are departed from their maisters to other places without testimonialls therefore quere what shalbe done hᵣin" (Ibid. I, 222).

(or, which is from our point of view practically the same thing, hiring someone else's servant without his prior consent) is, however, amply borne out by sessions records printed and unprinted.

In the North Riding in the early seventeenth century the offence was very common. There appear[1] to have been fifty-nine[2] presentments between 1605 and 1611, of which twelve[3] were at the January 1606-7 sessions, and fifteen[4] at that of January 1608-9. At a 1616 sessions there were eleven further presentments.[5] Thereafter cases were less numerous—three[6] in 1619, seven in the sixteen-twenties and thirties,[7] one in 1640,[8] 1655-6[9] and 1680-1.[10] The West Riding printed records, on the other hand, only yield two cases, in 1640[11] and 1641-2[12], the latter being of interest as illustrating that, as a servant hired without a testimonial was not lawfully retained, the parish of her employment was not responsible for providing relief; there are three East Riding examples in 1648 and 1651.[13] The Kesteven minutes only provide one instance, where a man had taken a servant into his house and incited him to leave his old service[14] —an offence in many respects indistinguishable from those under consideration. The records of Ipswich and Norwich suggest that action was quite usually taken in the first half of the seventeenth century—in the former there were at least twenty-three cases between 1618 and 1640,[15] in the

[1]The abbreviated form in which some of the entries are given makes it difficult to be certain.
[2]*N.R.Q.S.R.* I, 2, 33, 41, etc.
[3]*Ibid.* I, 60-1.
[4]*Ibid.* I, 143-4.
[5]*Ibid.* II, 118.
[6]*Ibid.* II, 190, 197, 213.
[7]*Ibid.* II, 239: III, 156, etc.
[8]*Ibid.* IV, 181.
[9]*Ibid.* V, 206.
[10]*Ibid.* VII, 44.
[11]*W.R.S. Records 1611-42,* 218.
[12]*Ibid.* 362.
[13]East Riding Q.S. Books, April 1648, Jan. 1650-1, April 1651.
[14]*Kesteven Q.S. Minutes,* 138.
[15]Ipswich Court Records: 1621 and 1631 were the peak years.

latter nine between 1615 and 1634.[1] At Norwich, rather
unusually, the emphasis was on punishing the servants
rather than the masters; on one occasion, for instance, a
master was given a fortnight to put away two male servants
whom he had lately received from London without testimonials, on pain of the statutory penalty of ten pounds, but
the two servants were to be committed and punished in
any case.[2] By 1660 the requirement of testimonials from
those seeking fresh employment had, a writer on the Middlesex records tells us, completely lapsed.[3] An attempt was,
however, made to revive it, a Proclamation of 1684 (the
only case in the printed Buckinghamshire records is of this
date[4]) having that purpose in view; only one Middlesex
indictment—ten years later—resulted, though there were
apparently some indictments for retaining other people's
servants.[5] The Gloucestershire justices made a belated
attempt to enforce the practice—in 1731 a printed order
relating to engaging servants without certificates was
posted throughout the county.[6]

Action in this latter instance was, there is reason to
believe, prompted by a desire to prevent an influx of those
likely to become chargeable. Probably the tendency of the
Norwich authorities to deal severely with servants so offending arose, in the same way, from a desire to dissuade those
from other parts coming to settle in the city (reference, it
will be remembered, was made earlier to their difficulties
with "foreign" feltmakers). Insistence on testimonials had,
of course, a very direct connection with problems of chargeability and relief, since the information they contained was
often instrumental in defining settlements. A further value
of the testimonial system is suggested by a paragraph in
Burn's *Justice of the Peace*, where he remarks that its lapse is

[1] Norwich Court Records.
[2] Norwich Court Records, Aug. 1625. Other Norwich instances of
punishment of servants offending in this way were given in an earlier
footnote.
[3] Dowdell, 147.
[4] *Bucks Sessions Records* I, 151, 159.
[5] Dowdell, 148.
[6] *E.H.R.* XLIII, 403.

responsible for the dearness of labour, since the fixing of wages in one county simply induces servants to move else-where. In other words, where wage assessment was being used to keep wages down, insistence on testimonials was a natural and necessary corollary. It does not, of course, follow that this particular aspect was the main reason for its inclusion in the Statute—the testimonial plan had many features to commend it. The "memorandum" of 1573 gives as its justification, as one might expect, the prevention of thieving and other "lewde Actes" by servants, for whom it is thereby made more difficult to depart with their masters' property and obtain other employment.[1] Masters who accepted servants without testimonials were, indeed, aiding and abetting servants in the desertion of their former masters, so that the two offences were, as suggested earlier, very close counterparts.[2] This is clearly brought out in a North Riding case where a certain William Eldridge was presented for refusing to serve Thomas Rowthe, and John Baines was presented at the same time for hiring Eldridge without a testimonial.[3] Where large numbers of servants are presented for departing unlawfully, and of masters for receiving servants without testimonials, there is naturally a presumption in favour of a labour shortage being the occasion of this law-breaking. In the North Riding in the years 1608-10, it will have been noticed, cases of offences of these two types appear alongside cases of paying or being paid more than the assessed rates. Insistence on testi-monials coupled with failure to raise the assessed rates to the required level would, of course, aggravate a labour shortage. In practice, despite the express application of a testimonial requirement (in this case a "temporary absence" certificate from a justice) to the case of harvesting in section sixteen, one would think it likely that even at its height, this requirement from persons entering was, in districts where

[1]Tawney and Power I, 362.
[2]In Devreux Edgar's Diary, though nothing is said about testi-monials, proceedings were taken against masters "abetting and har-bouring" servants who had run away.
[3]*N.R.Q.S.R.* II, 213.

labour was not too plentiful, relaxed.   On the other hand, even a temporary relaxation might lead to an influx of undesirables and those likely to become chargeable, a consideration which may well have been uppermost in the minds of the Hertfordshire justices when, in 1656, they drew up an order requiring constables to take up all travellers coming out of their country to work at hay-time and harvest without testimonials.[1]

If the voluntary departure of servants sometimes indicated that labour was scarce, the putting-away of servants by masters must sometimes, one would think, have been associated with a situation in which labour was becoming more plentiful.   Such putting-away, save in special circumstances, was illegal without the giving of a quarter's notice before the end of the term of hiring,[2] a forty-shilling fine being the penalty for infringement of this provision.[3]   In the printed and manuscript material examined, however, instances hardly occur in sufficient numbers to suggest widespread action on the part of masters similarly affected by some change in the labour market position.   Taking first straightforward cases, where no particular point of interest arises in connection with the entry, we find five[4] in the North Riding between 1606 and 1616, one in each of the years 1635,[5] 1669[6] and 1670,[7] and two in 1682.[8]   In Lincoln there was, in each of the three years 1658-60, an order requiring a master to take back a servant unlawfully put away;[9] there is a Lindsey instance in 1670,[10] a Holland case in 1676,[11] and three Kesteven cases in 1677,[12] 1678[13] and

[1]*Hertford C.R.* I, 116.
[2]5 Eliz. c. 4, sec. 4.
[3]5 Eliz. c. 4, sec. 6.
[4]*N.R.Q.S.R.* I, 37, 143, 202, 227: II, 119.
[5]*Ibid.* IV, 43.
[6]*Ibid.* VI, 136.
[7]*Ibid.* VI, 148.
[8]*Ibid.* VII, 54, 56.
[9]Lincoln Q.S. Minutes.
[10]Lindsey Q.S. Minutes.
[11]Holland Q.S. Minutes.
[12]*Kesteven Q.S. Minutes*, 62.
[13]*Ibid.* 92.

1692[1] respectively. There is a Norwich order requiring a
master to take back a servant he had unlawfully turned
away in 1656-7,[2] and two similar Suffolk orders in 1640-1
and 1641.[3] Suffolk provides a number of instances where
it is not stated whether the servant ran away or was put
away.[4] Some[5] of these cases arose, as might be expected,
in connection with possible chargeability, the point then
being not so much to determine whether master or servant
was to blame, as to send the servant back for the unexpired
part of his service and get him off your hands. The matter
often[6] came before the Court on complaint of the inhabitants of the parish to which the servant had gone after
leaving, or as a result of a periodic "diligent search" by
constables for newcomers likely to become chargeable.
Another common tendency was for cases of putting-away a
servant to be combined with detaining wages. There are
Suffolk examples in 1660,[7] 1702, 1703-4, 1705, 1710-11
and 1712,[8] while in Hertfordshire two cases in the seventeen-thirties show this dual character,[9] as does the only
Surrey instance mentioned in the printed records.[10] There
is a rather interesting Staffordshire case where turning-
away without just cause was combined both with detaining
wages and beating and wounding the servant. On this
occasion the difference was, by consent of both parties,
referred to Lady Littleton, but the master refused to abide
by her award; the Court, taking into consideration the
poverty of the servant, which meant inability to bring suit
against her master for recovery of her wages, ordered that

[1]*Kesteven Q. S. Minutes*, 421. There is one mention in *Manchester Sessions*, 106.
[2]Norwich Court Records, Feb. 1656–7.
[3]Suffolk Order Books, Jan. 1640–1: May 1641.
[4]*E.g. Ibid.* June 1641: Hilary 1659.
[5]*Ibid.* June 1642: Oct. 1644.
[6]*Ibid.* June 1645: Hilary 1658.
[7]*Ibid.* Easter 1660. Additional simple cases are to be found, October 1660 and April 1663.
[8]Devreux Edgar's Diary.
[9]*Hertford C.R.* VII, 238, 274. There is one other mention, *Ibid.* VI, 270.
[10]*Surrey Record Society* XIV.

Lady Littleton's award should stand and required the master to pay the wages detained, but apparently no action was taken against him in the matter of the assault or in that of his having turned away his servant without reasonable cause.[1] There is a Buckinghamshire case in 1685-6,[2] and Middlesex ones in 1683 and 1693—the Brentford justices, we are told, "were interesting themselves in the method of dismissal at this period".[3]

Turning to the more interesting border-line cases, in which the master was able to put forward some justification for sending his servant away, we find that, as a rule, the justices were willing to allow employers to dispense with the services of servants who had become physically incapable of performing their duties. This was so, at least, when a lame servant in the North Riding could not do his work,[4] when a Suffolk servant proved, after hiring, to be very infirm by reason of often being troubled with the falling sickness,[5] or another fell lunatic and lame.[6] Care had, however, to be taken that the business was done openly and in due legal form, as one Suffolk master found to his cost when, finding ten days after he hired a woman servant that she was so decrepit and sickly as to be unable to do her work, he complained to a justice, who sent her back by warrant to her previous place of settlement. The Court found that this warrant was obtained surreptitiously, and ordered that the woman be taken back to serve out her time.[7] Another master sent a woman servant who fell sick back to her father but, as she was likely to become chargeable there, she was sent back to the parish where, by her retainer, she had a settlement.[8] The Statute, of course, expressly said that the party grieved should complain,[9] and those who

[1] Staffs. Sessions Books, May 1621.
[2] *Bucks Sessions Records* I, 194.
[3] Dowdell, 147. There is an earlier case in *Middlesex C.R.* III, 34.
[4] *N.R.Q.S.R.* VII, 114.
[5] Suffolk Order Books, Jan. 1638–9.
[6] *Ibid.* Jan. 1644–5.
[7] *Ibid.* Hilary 1658.
[8] *Warwick C.R.* I, 173. In this instance it is not clear whether the overseers or her master provided for her.
[9] 5 Eliz. c. 4, sec. 4.

took the law into their own hands must expect, unless the justices were in lenient mood, to be saddled with a physically unfit servant until the end of the term of hiring, even if—as usually seemed to happen—they escaped being fined. Even greater care had, one may assume, to be taken when pregnancy was the cause of the servant's inability to perform her duties, since suspicion might easily fall on the master. In an early seventeenth-century North Riding case, for instance, where the servant alleged that the master was the father of her child, the Court imposed the fine of forty shillings for unlawfully putting her away.[1] Quite usually those discharging pregnant servants were ordered to take them back;[2] often "until the time for which she was retained expires, or until one month after her delivery, whichever is the sooner".[3] Sometimes, however, it was deemed a sufficient and reasonable cause.[4]

The procedure envisaged in the Act was, of course, that, instead of the servant departing or the master putting the servant away, the two of them should appear before a justice if any unforeseen difficulties arose, and should there by mutual consent (subject to his approval) bring their previous agreement to an end. Such discharges by mutual consent would seem, judging by a Suffolk magistrate's diary, to have been fairly common at the beginning of the eighteenth century. Sometimes a master, through ignorance or sympathy on the part of a justice, managed to obtain a discharge without his servant being consulted at all. When this was brought to the attention of the Court, however, such proceedings were likely to be pronounced invalid. Thus in one case of this type, where the servant had not been brought before the justice or given her consent, "the Court held Mr. Hunt's discharge under hand and seal was not good, the parties not being before him or by writing to him having signified their agreement, and that putting

[1] *N.R.Q.S.R.* I, 97.
[2] *Ibid.* III, 284: Suffolk Order Books, June 1650: *Hertford C.R.* V, 441.
[3] Suffolk Order Books, Jan. 1642–3: *N.R.Q.S.R.* II, 284.
[4] Suffolk Order Books, Jan. 1646–7.

his seal looked like a warrant or Judicial Act in him, whereas there is nothing required but a putting of the Justice's hand as an allowing".[1]

As to the reason for taking proceedings against those unlawfully discharging servants, the position is in many respects similar to that of the other offences discussed in this chapter. The 1573 "memorandum" alleges that servants turned away destitute or ill fall into evil ways and that stubborn servants, who can only be cured by correction, become still more stubborn if merely put away.[2] Dowdell, on the basis of the post-Restoration Middlesex records, says that "so far as there is any trace of a general object prompting the enforcement of annual contracts, it is the prevention of chargeability".[3] Where wage assessment was in operation, however, there were other reasons for insisting on annual contracts; these will be examined in the course of the next chapter.

Disputes between masters and servants, over the amount of wages due and other matters, were of very common occurrence, if the evidence of sessions records is to be believed. If the servant were hired at a chief constable's petty sessions, the wage to be received would be on record, which must have tended to simplify matters considerably. Failing this, if the good advice offered by the Shropshire justices[4] were followed, whereby the master was to reduce the terms of the agreement to writing in the presence of two witnesses, the same result would be achieved. However that may be, mention of wage disputes and of masters refusing to pay wages due is, on the whole, a great deal commoner than is mention of the other offences so far considered. Indeed, it is hardly possible to examine any book of sessions records without coming across material of this kind. This being so, any attempt to give a catalogue of cases of this type would be tedious, and all that need be

---

[1]Devreux Edgar's Diary, January 1712–13.
[2]Tawney and Power I, 361.
[3]Dowdell, 146.
[4]E.J. IV, 517.

done is to provide some indication of the nature of the information available.

Incidentally, a number of doubts exist as to the authority by which proceedings were taken by justices in this matter.[1] Where any statutory authority was given, it tended to be 5 Elizabeth c. 4, as in Brown's *Advice*,[2] or in a West Riding case where, on an employer declaring "that this Cort had no power to meddle with the wages of any servants or laborers", the matter was voted upon and "the whole Cort, not one voice dissenting, were of opinion that by the course and practize of this Cort cases of a like nature were every sessions determined, and that the same were warranted by the statute 5 Eliz. cap. 4, and that the very same pointe being formerly questioned and afterwards debated att the Councell Board . . . itt was approved as a legal proceeding".[3] Justices were, of course, expressly authorized to adjudge disputes between masters and servants where the departure of one of the parties was involved;[4] very often the detaining of his wages by his master was given by a servant as the reason for his departure; and, by a natural extension of authority, justices may have come to regard other disputes, not involving departure, as coming within their jurisdiction. Alternatively, it might be held that, since the terms of the contract were in doubt, it must be assumed that the assessed rates were operative;[5] and that, if the master refused to pay these rates, he was in some way infringing the justices' scale.[6] On one occasion the inability of one of the parties to sue the other for breach of contract at common law was even given by Quarter Sessions as justification—in view of the poverty of John Smith, he

[1]Dr. Peyton very kindly supplied me with some of the material on which the following paragraph is based.

[2]Brown, 348.

[3]*Yorks. Archæological Journal* V, 372.

[4]5 Eliz. c. 4, sec. 5.

[5]*Post*, 79.

[6]Burn, 625, quotes a judgment "tho' the statute gives them a power only to set the rate for wages, and not to order payment, yet grafting hereupon, they have also taken upon them to order payment, and the Courts of law are indulgent in remedies for wages".

"not being able to prosecute his suit at common law against the said Thomas Wells for his said wages, that the consideration hereof shall be referred to a justice";[1] similar justification (the poverty of the petitioner) was given in a Staffordshire case quoted earlier in this chapter.[2] None of these grounds seems altogether satisfactory, though the justices themselves might (and, when they gave as their authority 5 Elizabeth c. 4, evidently did) regard them as adequate. Fortunately, however, Holdsworth has very recently explained how a case of 1598 (following precedents based on statutes repealed by 5 Elizabeth c. 4), which "laid it down that if a person was compelled to serve he could bring an action on the Statute for his wages, and was not driven to sue by action of debt", led to the view being taken that *if a person was compelled to serve in husbandry*, he could apply to a magistrate if his master detained his wages.[3] This, of course, explains why the justices' power to act in the matter was sometimes challenged on the ground that the wages in dispute were not for work in husbandry.[4] In the West Riding case we have noticed, however, the magistrates do not seem to have been any the less emphatic about their right to interfere because the wages involved were for charcoal carrying;[5] while in Burn we find that "orders have been held good, where it did not appear that the service was in husbandry, for the Court said they would intend it so, unless the contrary appeared".[6] The majority of cases given in a Suffolk justice's diary relate to wages in husbandry, but warrants were occasionally issued in connection with the detaining of wages for work not coming within this category.[7] At all events, the justices' activity seems (given the complaints) to have been spontaneous, in

[1] *Warwick C.R.* I, 76.
[2] *Ante*, 43–4.
[3] Holdsworth XI, 467–8.
[4] *E.g.* Burn, 625: *Justice's Case Law*, 294.
[5] Perhaps this was counted as husbandry.
[6] Burn, 625.
[7] Devreux Edgar's Diary, March 1701–2, January 1702–3. The Middlesex magistrates, too, seem sometimes to have ignored the husbandry restriction (Dowdell, 153).

the sense, at least, that we do not know of pressure having been brought to bear on them from above in this connection. In the eighteenth century, more definite statutory authority was provided for recovery of wages; and, in legislation of that century applying assessment to particular trades, the mistake of omission made in the Statute of Artificers was not repeated, for special provision was made to deal with the detaining of wages.[1]

Turning to the cases themselves, the North Riding records, though not providing as many instances as might have been expected, illustrate the procedure often followed. Thus in January 1663-4 a New Malton yeoman was presented for refusing to pay three pounds to his servant for a year's service. The Court ordered that the matter be referred to two justices, and at the next sessions we find an order that the master pay his servant two pounds in satisfaction of his wages.[2] North Riding cases appear to have been most numerous during the sixteen-fifties;[3] there is an East Riding instance in 1650 also.[4] In Holland and Kesteven, on the other hand (where records are, however, missing for earlier periods), the seventies and eighties provided cases at every sessions,[5] sometimes five or six at a time.[6] The records of Nottinghamshire,[7] Staffordshire,[8] Northamptonshire,[9] Suffolk,[10] Hertfordshire,[11] Buckinghamshire,[12] Middlesex,[13] Kent,[14] Surrey,[15] Worcester,[16]

[1]Holdsworth XI, 471, 473.
[2]N.R.Q.S.R. VI, 75–7.
[3]E.g. Ibid. V, 137, 151, 175, 188.
[4]East Riding Q.S. Books, July 1650.
[5]Holland Q.S. Minutes from 1673: Kesteven Q.S. Minutes, 9, 10, 14, 20, etc.
[6]E.g. Kesteven Q.S. Minutes, 61–2, 119.
[7]Copnall, 67.
[8]E.g. Staffs. Sessions Books, 1626, 1628.
[9]Northants Q.S. Records, 193.
[10]Suffolk Order Books.
[11]Hertford C.R. V, 107, 147, etc.
[12]Bucks. Sessions Records I, 61.
[13]E.g. Middlesex Sessions Records I, 8, 453.
[14]E.H.R. XLIII, 401–2.
[15]E.g. Surrey Record Society XIV, 45.
[16]Worcs. C.R., 235.

Wiltshire,[1] Gloucester[2] and Somerset[3] all contain examples, though not in as great quantity as the Lincolnshire records.[4] The astonishing number of cases recorded in a Suffolk justice's diary[5] suggests that, if we had similar information regarding the activities of justices out of sessions in other parts of the country and for other periods, the issuing of warrants requiring masters to pay wages detained from their servants or else appear and show cause to the contrary, would prove to be one of the most important parts of a magistrate's business, and certainly much more important (in terms of number of cases dealt with) than any of the offences coming directly under the Statute of Artificers. The legal costs involved in obtaining redress must, of course, have meant that in many other cases of which we have no record, servants were unable to get the wages due to them.[6] That the authorities did not always ignore this difficulty is, however, to be inferred from a number of examples of attempts to overcome it in different parts of the country. Thus in Suffolk on one occasion, as it appeared to the Court that a complainant had been at great expense both in fees to the Clerk of the Peace for orders and in payment for warrants, his master was ordered not merely to pay the wages due but also fourteen shillings extra;[7] while on two[8] later occasions the three shillings for the order was charged to the offending master, in one[9] case the servant being discharged of her service as well (there is another instance of this latter being done in the Buckinghamshire records[10]). In Buckinghamshire, indeed, steps of this kind seem to have been taken more often than elsewhere

---

[1]*H.M.C. Various* I, 152.
[2]*E.H.R.* XLIII, 401–2.
[3]*Somerset Q.S. Records* IV, 4.
[4]There were, however, 21 cases in Gloucestershire 1716–91, *E.H.R.* XLIII, 401–2.
[5]*Devreux Edgar's Diary.*
[6]*Cf.* Dowdell, 153–4.
[7]Suffolk Order Books, June 1645.
[8]*Ibid.* Easter 1660: Oct. 1660.
[9]*Ibid.* Easter 1660.
[10]*Bucks. Sessions Records* I, 201.

—the costs of appealing (amounting in one[1] case to
£1 14s. 4d.) were usually[2] added to the wages to be paid,
and masters were sometimes imprisoned[3] or fined[4] for dis-
regarding orders, though when a magistrate, Sir Dennis
Hampson, was at fault, the Clerk of the Peace was
instructed[5] to write to him signifying the resentment of the
Court concerning his carriage in the matter—in relation,
presumably, to the Court, not his servant—this letter pro-
ducing the desired effect.[6] A Warwickshire order of 1629
refers a wage dispute to a justice as, in view of the poverty
of the claimant, he was not able "to prosecute his suit at
common law",[7] a Shropshire wages order of 1702 is to be
paid for,[8] while a Somerset order of 1676 requires William
Curry to pay to James Orchard a sum due to him for wages,
plus twenty shillings for his expenses in recovering them,
"as the Court is informed that Curry has confessed the debt
was due to Orchard, but said that he would not pay the
same until he had put him to some expense".[9]

A rather interesting instance illustrating the awareness
of individual justices of the need for some effective method
of recovery of wages without cost to the claimant is provided by a note in a Suffolk magistrate's diary. In this
note he explains why, in the case of many of the complaints
of servants "against masters present and masters lately
gone from, the first by misusage either in diet or beating and
the latter from not paying of their wages when gone away"
he has not granted warrants against the masters concerned.
His main reason, he asserts, was a desire not to put complainants to any charge for warrants; with this end in view
he tried as often as possible to adopt the method of sending
a note to the master earnestly pressing him to take the

[1] *Bucks. Sessions Records* I, 276.
[2] *Ibid.* I, 4, 16, 57, 276.
[3] *Ibid.* I, 52.
[4] *Ibid.* I, 18.
[5] *Ibid.* I, 471.
[6] *Ibid.* I, 493.
[7] *Warwick C.R.* I, 76.
[8] *Salop C.R.* I, 199.
[9] *Somerset Q.S. Records* IV, 210.

matter into his serious consideration and do justice to his servant. Had he kept a clerk in his house as other justices did, the servant might, in his opinion, have been made to pay as much for the note as if it had been a warrant; but by dispensing with the services of a clerk, and adopting the note procedure, he claimed to be obtaining redress for servants in a large proportion of cases without any cost to them whatever. He adds, incidentally, that a further advantage of this procedure lay in the fact that only too often masters brought by warrants before justices had a grudge against complainants for bringing them into disgrace in this manner, and usually managed to obtain their revenge at some later date; by only using the method of warrants, therefore, as a last resort, this disadvantage was also got over.[1]

As to the significance of the widespread failure of masters to pay wages due, and of the attempts to force them to do so, a satisfactory answer cannot yet be supplied. If the cases had, in any district, been mainly confined to one or two years, one might have guessed that masters who had taken on servants at high wages during a temporary labour shortage were reluctant to pay these wages when the time came, but an explanation of this kind will hardly meet this particular case. The editor of the printed Oxfordshire Sessions Records remarks "on the much-argued question as to how far the wages rates that Quarter Sessions decreed were enforced, some light is thrown by entries [ordering payment of wages due to servants]".[2] It is not, however, clear whether by this she means merely that the actual rates given in these orders are of interest for comparison with the assessed rates, or something more than this. I cannot help feeling myself that material relating to the non-payment of wages is less helpful, from the point of view of the assessment of wages, than the other types of case considered in this and the following chapter.

[1]Devreux Edgar's Diary.
[2]Gretton, 6–7.

CHAPTER IV

COMPLEMENTARY PARTS OF THE POLICY: II

THE information which was at the disposal of Quarter
Sessions regarding the extent to which different
sections of the Statute of Artificers were being observed did
not, of course, any more than information connected with
the operation of other statutes, come in altogether spon-
taneously. The presentments normally found in sessions
records are, as is well known, of rather mixed origin, some
being in effect answers to written questions, some being on
the initiative of constables themselves, and some being
matters within the Grand Jury's own knowledge. This
being so, scarcity of cases connected with the assessment of
wages may, where it is met with, be partly due to lack of
interest on the part of the justices in enforcing these particular sections of the Statute. We may, for instance, think
it significant that none of the seventeen "articles" to which
Oxfordshire constables in the late seventeenth century were
required to furnish answers[1] had anything to do with the
subject of this study, since these articles represented a
catalogue of those matters on which, at that time, the central
government and the justices required their agents to exercise particular vigilance. On the other hand, the frequency
with which wage assessments were accompanied by instructions[2] to constables suggests that they were intended to be
enforced, (though one sometimes wonders whether the very
inclusion of these instructions may have signified that constables were not as familiar with their functions under this

---

[1]Gretton, p. lxvi.
[2]*E.g. E.H.R.* LII, 283, 285. In the West Riding these instructions
grew steadily longer, *E.J.* XXIV, 229-30.

as under other statutes). As against this, however, it has
to be remembered that provision was made, both in the
Statute itself and subsequently, for additional assemblies to
secure the smooth operation of the labour code, and that
records of proceedings at these assemblies have not often
come down to us. There were, to begin with, the chief
constables' petty sessions, to be discussed shortly. Secondly,
the justices in their several divisions were expected to meet
twice a year to see that the Act was duly executed.[1] Thirdly,
instructions were issued in 1605[2] requiring that justices
should assemble themselves together by divisions once
(about mid-time) between every general sessions of the
peace, to inquire of and see the due execution of, *inter alia*,
the Statute of Artificers. Fourthly, the "Book of Orders"
issued in 1631,[3] directed justices to give monthly accounts
of their proceedings to the sheriffs and to hold monthly
meetings in their divisions in order to exercise a closer
supervision over the administration of the poor laws; in all
probability certain aspects of 5 Elizabeth c. 4 were considered at these monthly meetings.[4] There were, in addition, special arrangements in different counties which may,
or may not, have represented attempts to comply with one
or other of these provisions. These included the North
Riding additional summer sessions to hear cases under the
Act,[5] the Devonshire district sub-committees of the early
seventeenth century,[6] and the Warwick sessions "holden
to enquire here and determyn causes towching Artificers
laborers and Apprentices . . . In wch chardge was given to
the Jury to determyn and present matters conteyned in
c^rten artycles delivred to them";[7] while the Buckingham-

---

[1] 5 Eliz. c. 4, sec. 30.
[2] Gretton, pp. xxvi-xxvii.
[3] *Warwick C.R.* I, p. xxix.
[4] Miss Hindmarsh found that monthly meetings were regularly
held in Hertfordshire, Sussex, Lancashire, Warwickshire, Nottinghamshire, Derbyshire, Staffordshire, Somersetshire and Worcestershire.
[5] *N.R.Q.S.R.* I, 204.
[6] Hewins, 85.
[7] *Book of John Fisher*, 156.

shire "governors of labourers" for every township, mentioned in the regulations following the wage assessment of
1561, were intended to ensure the execution of the statutes
relating to labourers then in force.[1] When it is realized
how much of this activity we have now no record of, it is
clear that it would be unwise too hastily to assume that, at
a given date in a given district, nothing was being done to
secure the observance of the Statute, unless strong corroborative evidence existed. It is, of course, true that—
except in so far as they were additional general sessions held
at a time other than the four regular dates—these meetings
did not have the character of sessions, since petty sessions
in any modern sense cannot (as the editor of the Oxfordshire Sessions Records has recently adduced valuable
additional evidence to show)[2] be regarded as having
originated any earlier than the eighteenth century. Nevertheless, even a single justice could, *inter alia*, order the idle
able-bodied to work, punish vagabonds, order committal
to Bridewell, and adjudge controversies between servants
and masters;[3] cases beyond the competence of one or two
justices could be passed on to sessions; and the "assemblies"
possessed the added advantage that they provided the
justices with additional means of getting to know, from chief
and petty constables, how prevalent—short of the actual
formulation of presentments—infringements of the Statute
were, and whether, for instance, some alteration in the
justices' scale or the more vigorous application of the
existing scale would best meet the case. One may, in fact,
assume that causes of friction were quite usually eliminated
in this way, so that it may often have been only a small
percentage of the difficulties that appeared in the sessions
records we know. Account should, at all events, be taken
of the functions this additional machinery was intended to
perform before finally attaching any special significance,
for instance, to the complete absence of cases having to do

[1]Tawney and Power I, 336–7.
[2]Gretton, p. lxxiv.
[3]Gretton (quoting Dalton), pp. x-xi.

with our aspect of the Statute in the volume of Hampshire
indictments and presentments 1646-1660,[1] or of "pro-
secutions on any of the possible counts under the Statute of
Apprentices"[2] in the Warwickshire records, or the finding
of only one case relevant to this study (leaving before term)
in a search of half-a-dozen volumes of West Riding indictment books.[3] Even in a case where ignorance of the procedure to be followed is found, as when the East Riding
justices in 1647 instructed the Clerk of the Peace to certify
the rates of wages up above and procure Proclamations
thereupon, there must have been rates to certify or the order
would have had no meaning.[4]

One of these types of assembly would seem, because of
its peculiar importance in the whole functioning of wage
assessment, to demand separate treatment here, and that
despite the admitted difficulty that, as one recent writer
remarks, "it was a Court with a history, but of which little
is known".[5] This type is, of course, the chief constable's
petty or statute sessions. The commonest offence connected with statute sessions recorded in the North Riding
sessions records is failure to appear. In one year, July
1608 to April 1609, no fewer than twenty petty constables
were presented for not appearing at statute or petty
sessions;[6] there had been nine such presentments earlier,[7]
and there was one later in 1609,[8] followed by six in 1611,[9]
(of whom one constable obstinately refused to make a presentment at a petty sessions, "by reason he was to goe to a
horse-race"). Thereafter, however, presentments were
fewer in number—five in 1612-13,[10] three in 1614,[11] two in

[1]Furley, 106–7.
[2]Ashby, 174.
[3]*E.J.* XXIV, 230–1.
[4]East Riding Q.S. Books, October 1647.
[5]*Kesteven Q.S. Minutes*, p. xliv.
[6]*N.R.Q.S.R.* I, 112–3, 127, 131, 137, 142, 151–2.
[7]*Ibid.* I, 24, 33, 46, 56, 92, 112.
[8]*Ibid.* I, 159.
[9]*Ibid.* I, 212, 214, 232, 238.
[10]*Ibid.* II, 9.
[11]*Ibid.* II, 42.

1618[1] and two in 1619[2]—after which there would appear to be no further mention of the matter. In only two of the cases mentioned is there any doubt as to whether the person presented was a constable. At a midsummer sessions in Kesteven a constable was indicted for failing to deliver his bill of all servants at a statute sessions of the previous October,[3] while another North Riding case had involved a constable refusing to make presentment of the masters and servants and their wages.[4] It is fairly clear, therefore, that where statute sessions were in effective operation the attendance of petty constables was obligatory, and that the purpose of their presence there was to make presentment of those offending against 5 Elizabeth c. 4. and certain other statutes, and to deliver their bills setting forth the names of masters and their servants and the wages they were paid in their several parishes. The North Riding justices issued instructions that those petty constables not appearing at the petty sessions to make presentments should themselves be presented by the high constables,[5] and there is reference on one occasion to five-shilling fines having been imposed,[6] though one man (who may not have been a constable) who submitted was only fined sixpence.[7] Fines for negligence of this type seem to have varied widely. In the Grimsby records we find constables being fined ten shillings for non-appearance at statute sessions in 1637 and 1638, twenty shillings in 1645 and 1646, two-and-sixpence in 1650, five shillings in 1653 ("for neglecting to return his bill at this sessions") and ten shillings in 1655 ("for neglecting of his office at this court")[8]. Mere attendance was not in itself sufficient, for there is a case of a constable who appeared at a petty sessions but was presented for departing without leave,

[1]N.R.Q.S.R. II, 186.
[2]Ibid. II, 209.
[3]Kesteven Q.S. Minutes, 466.
[4]N.R.Q.S.R. I, 248.
[5]Ibid. II, 206–7.
[6]Ibid. I, 92.
[7]Ibid. I, 24.
[8]Great Grimsby Court Records.

not having made any presentment;[1] while the "bills" presented had to be complete.[2]

Failure of masters to appear might also, however, be treated as an offence. Thus no fewer than one hundred and twenty people were presented at one Holland sessions for failure to appear at statute sessions to hear the assessed rates and hire their servants according to law,[3] two Northamptonshire yeomen and seven husbandmen were on one occasion presented for not appearing and recording their servants that they hired at statute sessions,[4] while an entry in the seventeen-twenties in a Suffolk book of precedents and indictments suggests that failure to attend at statute sessions and hire your servants there was still regarded as an offence.[5] Where the East Yorkshire practice was followed of having a roll call of masters,[6] offenders could easily be detected. In the same category, from our point of view, are the many Nottinghamshire presentments we are told of for hiring servants outside statute sessions, (including twenty-eight in July 1616 for retaining servants out of petty sessions and not recording them, and nineteen the following January for not recording the names of their servants in the books of the chief constable)[7], the present- ment of three North Riding husbandmen for not recording the names and salaries of their servants before the chief constable at the time of hiring,[8] and the fining of two masters one-and-sixpence a piece at a Kesteven sessions in 1695 for failure to hire their servants at the chief constable's petty sessions.[9] Clearly, the master's legal duty was not performed merely by hiring his servants at the appropriate place and time; he had, in addition, to record the bargain in the chief constable's book which—take in conjunction

[1]N.R.Q.S.R. I, 24.
[2]Ibid. VII, 41: Northants Q.S. Records, 62.
[3]Holland Q.S. Minutes, Midsummer 1676 (Spalding).
[4]Northants Q.S. Records, 62.
[5]Book of Precedents and Indictments, 89.
[6]Farming Books of Henry Best, 135.
[7]Copnall, 66.
[8]N.R.Q.S.R. I, 27.
[9]Kesteven Q.S. Minutes, 486.

with the proclamation of the assessed rates, and the penalties
for infringing them, at that assembly—would, it was hoped,
ensure that no over-payment took place. On the other
hand if, for some reason, a hiring did not take place at the
appointed place and time, the master was expected to
record the details with the authorities also, and was liable
to be presented if he failed to do so. The periodic[1] visit of
the petty constable to take a note of details regarding
masters, servants and wages for entry in his "bill" provided
a final means of checking-up, as it were, those bargains
which had somehow failed to be recorded elsewhere. We
are probably justified in inferring from a North Yorkshire
case, when a woman refused "to give the names of her
servants, nor tickets nor rates of her servants",[2] that these
periodic visits were sometimes used to determine whether
testimonials had been duly produced at the time of hiring.
The Ipswich justices instructed constables in September
1575 to make what appears to have been a special search
for all newcomers, and to certify to the bailiffs when and for
what such servants were retained, and at what wages.[3]
Presentments for refusal to supply the necessary information
are, in the North Riding in the early part of the century,
fairly numerous. Two parishes were collectively presented
for refusing to give the names of servants and their wages
to the constables or the head constables[4] and, in the four
years 1606-10, there were twelve cases of individuals being
presented for this offence,[5] or for failing or refusing to
register or record wages and names[6] (whether this latter
referred to the periodic visits of the petty constable, or to
statute sessions, is not clear). Failure to record details at
statute sessions may sometimes have been due to the charge
of a penny a servant made for this. The high constables in
the West Riding, we are told, "doe call in once or twice a

[1] In the West Riding, twice-yearly: *E.J.* XXIV, 230.
[2] *N.R.Q.S.R.* I, 99.
[3] Ipswich Court Records, Sept. 1575.
[4] *N.R.Q.S.R.* I, 60.
[5] *Ibid.* I, 60, 69, 99.
[6] *Ibid.* I, 71, 98, 105, 148, 163, 188.

year by warrantes all the servantes within their wapen-
tackes, and comaund them to appeare before them to enter
their names, their wages, there tearme for which they are
hyred, and take a penny a piece for this of every servant".[1]
Whether the servants themselves paid in the West Riding or
not, in the North Riding it is the masters who are presented
for refusing to pay a penny to the head constable for entering servants' wages in their book according to the custom.[2]
Henry Best's remarks on the hiring of servants in the East
Riding throw additional light on this aspect of the matter;
it would appear that the charge of one penny only applied
where servants were hired for an additional year. At
statute sessions "if the master will not sette him att liberty,
then the cheife constable is to lette them knowe what wages
the statute will allowe, and to sette downe a reasonable and
indifferent wage betwixt them, and hee is to have one
penny of the master for every servant that stayeth two yeares
in a place, or is not sette att liberty, and this the pettie
constables are to doe for him, viz: to sende in bills of the
names of all such servants as stay with theire olde masters,
and to gather the money, and sende it him".[3] In any case,
masters who proposed to pay servants more than the
assessed rates would naturally be reluctant to have the
details entered in the high constable's book; while one
would probably be justified in guessing that failure to comply with the law in some respect (private hiring, overpayment, not requiring the production of a testimonial, or
hiring for a shorter period than one year) was usually the
reason for refusal to provide the petty constable on demand
with names and other information regarding servants
employed. There are a few[4] later North Riding cases of
refusal to certify or record such information, but none of
these is later than 1621.

To return, however, to a consideration of those whose
attendance at statute sessions was obligatory, it naturally

[1]*W.R.S. Records 1611-42*, 396.
[2]Four instances, *N.R.Q.S.R.* I, 60, 143.
[3]*Farming Books of Henry Best*, 135.
[4]*N.R.Q.S.R.* I, 207, 248-9: II, 13, 234: III, 111.

followed that, if masters were successfully persuaded to go there, servants' attendance would be required also. We have already seen that it was customary for the West Riding high constables to command servants to appear before them once or twice a year; there has to be added to this the presentment, in Northamptonshire in 1630, of seven labourers for not appearing at statute sessions[1]—the only case of its kind which appears to have survived. The attendance of justices at these sessions was not (except in some counties)[2] essential. Where one or two of them did attend, the assembly presumably possessed the competence of a single justice. In Essex, however, a jury was appointed.[3] Cowell speaks of statute sessions as being for the debating of differences between masters and their servants, the rating of servants' wages and "the bestowing of such people in Service, as being fit to serve, either refuse to seek, or cannot get Masters;" whether it was even possible to go as far as this without the presence of a justice is not, however, stated.

The purpose of all this is not a matter of doubt. Both the holding of statute sessions to which those concerned had to come, and the periodic visits of the petty constables to householders, were clearly intended, in the first place, to make private hiring, retaining servants without testimonials, paying more than the assessed rates, and so on more difficult. Secondly, they were intended to acquaint people who might genuinely be in doubt, with the rates in the justices' scale; thirdly, they were intended to provide the justices with information regarding the price that labour of different kinds was commanding, and the extent to which the Statute was being observed; with, finally, the functions mentioned in the previous paragraph—adjusting the simpler differences between master and servant, and finding masters for those who were unable or unwilling to find them for themselves. Private hiring it was desirable to eliminate for a whole variety of reasons—it probably meant

[1] *Northants Q.S. Records*, 62.
[2] *E.g.* Nottinghamshire (Copnall, 12); Grimsby (Great Grimsby Court Records); Suffolk (Devreux Edgar's Diary).
[3] Hindmarsh, 122.

disregard of the assessed rates and of whether the servant
had lawfully departed from his last master; it was liable to
make disputes between the parties over the terms of hiring
difficult to settle, it might lead to confusion later in appeals
touching settlements.[1] How far it was possible to prevent
such hiring is, however, doubtful. Despite such disadvantages as having no redress if your servant ran away,[2]
private hiring seems to have been fairly common even at
an early period, and to have been countenanced (at
least in some districts) provided the details were recorded.
Thus the Norwich Records, for instance, contain entries
regarding the retaining of servants on the following dates in
1615—3rd May, 12th and 15th July, 11th November, and
9th December; again, in 1630 there were entries on 2nd
October, 13th November and 29th December.[3] On the
other hand, a Hertfordshire draft order of 1656 suggests a
more rigid interpretation of the Statute. It is there provided
that in case of death or other extraordinary occasion a
servant may repair, along with the master wishing to retain
him, to the high constable's register and obtain a certificate
of hiring which is to be as effectual as if the hiring had been
done at the set statute.[4]

The importance of retaining servants for a year is, of
course, closely linked up with the considerations under discussion. Ideally, if one statute sessions were held in each
district every year, and if all hiring were done there, idleness and vice would have been much reduced,[5] masters
would have been able to get their servants at fair prices
(in relation to the available supply), and infringements of
the Statute would have been at a minimum. In practice the
holding of two statute sessions per hundred per year
seems to have been quite a usual custom,[6] though there

[1]*E.J.* IV, 517.
[2]*Hertford C.R.* VI, 346.
[3]Norwich Court Records.
[4]*Hertford C.R.* I, 116.
[5]Tawney and Power I, 360.
[6]Constables to keep petty sessions twice every year (Ipswich Court
Records, Nov. 1578): *W.R.S. Records 1611-42*, 396.

are signs that one a year became a commoner practice later on,[1] or two within a week or so of each other.[2] Henry Best records that in East Yorkshire in the first half of the seventeenth century "there are usually two, and sometimes three, sittinges or statute-dayes for every division, whereof the first is a weeke or more afore Martynmasse, and the next three or fower dayes after that"; the towns called to the earlier sitting had the best of this arrangement.[3] It rather looks, from the dates of petty sessions in the North Riding,[4] as though they were held in such a way as not to clash with each other—perhaps so that masterless men and servantless masters could have several opportunities of satisfying their needs; this was definitely not the case, however, in the East Riding in the eighteenth century, for the chief constables for the several divisions were ordered to hold their petty sessions on the same day.[5] The case of Holland is of considerable interest as giving us some clue to the reasons behind the insistence of the authorities on a particular number of statute sessions being held. In 1688, when confirming the existing assessed rates, the justices there ordered that privy sessions be kept only once a year.[6] In 1726, however, a petition of householders and other substantial persons was presented explaining that, although the original decision to hold statute sessions in each division only once a year had been intended to reduce the exorbitant demands of servants, this decision had had precisely the contrary effect—"since the making of the said order servants were become more scarce and the same seemed rather to serve to enhance the rates and wages of servants". Accordingly, the justices agreed that the earlier order should be rescinded and that "the Chief Constables of each Division have

[1] At Thetford 1755–66, some time in September (Thetford Court Books); once a year was the practice in the East Riding in the 1720's.
[2] To be held in every district, 1724, on 16th and 26th October (V.C.H. Notts. II, 295–6). A similar arrangement held good in Suffolk (Devreux Edgar's Diary).
[3] Farming Books of Henry Best, 134–5.
[4] E.g. N.R.Q.S.R. I, 24, 46, 92 : II, 123.
[5] East Riding Order Books, June 1722, October 1723.
[6] Holland Q.S. Minutes, Easter 1688 (Kirton).

liberty to hold Statutes as often as there shall be occasion
for the service of the country, at such times and seasons in
the year as the Law appoints and is customary for these purposes"; petty constables were particularly required to
execute warrants in connection with the holding of such
sessions, and to see "that peace and order be duly observed
during the same".[1] Local variations in all matters connected with statute sessions, which were older than the
Act, were expressly provided for in it.[2] Insistence on contracts being for a year, in the interests of stable and regular
employment[3] and for reasons connected with chargeability,[4]
or simply as a necessary corollary to statute sessions and
wage assessment—for without annual contracts, private
hiring and the arrangement of bargains not in conformity
with the assessed rates would very probably have resulted[5]
—must usually, however, have taken the form of proceedings against servants leaving, or masters putting-away
before term, rather than proceedings against masters
engaging servants (in husbandry and the enumerated
occupations) for less than a year, for the latter are very
rarely met with.   The Ipswich justices, it is true, issued
instructions in 1578 to constables that they should from
time to time in their sessions and searches see that no
servant was retained for less term than one whole year, a
special search being undertaken forthwith for that purpose;[6]
while there were, in Warwick in 1586, several presentments
of glovers for retaining men to work with them by the day
contrary to the Statute,[7] and three tailors were in 1609 in

[1]Holland Q.S. Minutes, Easter 1726 (Kirton). Massingberd, while
mentioning the first of these orders (*V.C.H. Lincs.* II, 338) omits all
reference to the second and more interesting one.
[2]5 Eliz. c. 4, sec. 40.
[3]*V.S.W.* XI, 312.
[4]Dowdell, 146.
[5]The Suffolk justices were definitely of the opinion that the reason
for the Act's insistence on contracts being for a year was "to prevent
Clandestine settlements between Master and servant", and acted on
this assumption when doubts arose as to whether a particular hiring
had in fact been for a year (Devreux Edgar's Diary, January 1712–13).
[6]Ipswich Court Records, Nov. 1578.
[7]*Book of John Fisher*, 161.

North Yorkshire presented for taking wages by the day "contrary to the Statute sett downe by the Justices";[1] but that is apparently all. At Hedon, Yorkshire, it looks as though hiring for less than a year was allowed, provided the matter was put on record and the end of the term was Mayday or Martinmas, so that the same difficulty need not arise again; this, at least, would seem a reasonable interpretation of two entries on an otherwise blank page of a sessions book—"11 November 1663, M.B. hath hired herself to A.D. until Mayday next, twenty shillings wages, twelve-pence earnest penny: 31 December 1664, S.D. hired until Martinmas next, twenty-five shillings and twelve-pence earnest".[2] Hiring for less than a year meant, of course (as in the case of private unrecorded hiring, or overpayment, or accepting a servant without a testimonial), that neither party had any redress if the other failed to carry out the terms of the agreement, since the contract was void from the beginning and carried with it the further disadvantage that the retainer, being void, did not confer a settlement.[3]

This completes our survey of complementary parts of Elizabethan labour policy. Logically, of course, our net ought to have been cast sufficiently wide to include many other aspects of that policy, such as poor relief or action in regard to enclosures. Some may feel that, at the very least, an attempt should have been made to examine the extent to which the Statute 31 Elizabeth c.7, was enforced. How far, for instance, was the rule that cottages must, with certain exceptions, have four acres of land, used to prevent an influx of those likely to become chargeable;[4] or the provision against the taking of inmates by cottagers

---

[1] *N.R.Q.S.R.* I, 148. Tailors were only included amongst those who must be hired for a year in the later stages of the bill's progress (Tawney and Power I, 335).

[2] Hedon Sessions Books. *Cf.* Great Grimsby Court Books.

[3] *E.g.* Suffolk Order Books, Sept. 1650—"X was never lawfully settled as a hired servant, but only did labour there with several inhabitants by the week".

[4] As, for instance, in Chester in 1596 (Morris, 452).

alternately relaxed and enforced according as a desire to relieve a labour scarcity or to keep down the poor rates predominated? Perhaps on another occasion it will prove possible to make such an attempt.

CHAPTER V

THE COST-OF-LIVING ASPECT

A S is well known, the Statute of Artificers contained, in its opening words, the justification for altering the existing law that the statutory rates of wages then in force had, owing to the advance of prices which had taken place since their enactment, become inapplicable; while, in the section[1] dealing with the assessment of wages, it was expressly laid down that the justices should call to them such discreet and grave persons as they thought fit, and should confer together respecting the plenty or scarcity of the time and other circumstances. What light do the assessments themselves throw on the problem as to whether the justices did, in fact, make the cost-of-living a major factor in determining assessment?

There are, firstly, statements included in the actual wording of assessments as to the reason for altering the justices' rates. These, though not necessarily to be taken at their face value, can be accepted as evidence of a kind. (They are not to be confused, of course, with mere recitations of the opening words of the Statute itself which nearly all the early, and some of the late, assessments contain). The earliest instances are to be found in the 1563 assessments. Thus in a rature for the city of Lincoln the prices of wheat, rye, malt, beans, pease and barley, mutton, veal, beef, eggs, butter and cheese are given at the outset as having been taken into account, together with other necessaries and victuals being very dear,[2] while Holland and Rutland assessments of the

[1] 5 Eliz. c. 4, sec. 11.
[2] V.C.H. Lincs. II, 330.

same year speak of great prices and dearth.[1] A Chester assessment of 1570 mentions the *cheapness* of necessaries.[2] In the Canterbury rature of 1576 it is stated that "the causes and concyd [erations] why the said Mayor, Aldermen, and Shyryffes, have rated and taxed the wages and rates above said, is onely the dearth of vitayles, cloth, and other necessaries, which at this pre [sent are] so scarce and deare within the sayde Citie, that poore men are not able at reasonable price to at [tayn t]heyr necessaries".[3] Ten years later the Lord Mayor and certain London justices had "an especiall consideracion and regard unto the high and verie chargeable prices of all kinde of victualls, fewell rayment and apparrell bothe linnen and wollen and alsoe of howsrente, and other especiall and accidentall charges" wherewith artificers and labourers living in the city were burdened.[4] In 1597 a Chester assessment referred to "the great dearth and scarsitie of things at this present."[5] The Somerset justices in the sixteen-forties asked the Grand Jury to present their opinions what wages they thought fit to be assessed, "respect beinge hadd to the present tymes";[6] that this was not a mere form of words was suggested by the statement that, in 1648, the rates "for such as find themselves are raised in regard to the greate price of all sortes of provision att this present".[7] The Essex assessment of 1651 is said to have been made having a special regard to prices of victuals and apparel and other necessary charges "wherewith artificers, labourers and servants have been grieviously charged with than in time past".[8] (In Derbyshire, incidentally, we are told that during the years of the Commonwealth the justices were far fairer in their statute wages than at any other period).[9] In

[1] *Tudor and Stuart Proclamations* I, 61.
[2] Hindmarsh, 158.
[3] *Tudor and Stuart Proclamations* I, 75.
[4] Tawney and Power I, 366.
[5] Morris, 367.
[6] *Somerset Q.S. Records* III, 40.
[7] *Ibid.* III, 67. In fact, however, only one such rate was raised.
[8] Rogers, *History* VI, 694.
[9] Cox II, 242.

1655 we get the first mention (apart from the Chester instance in 1570) of scaling wages downwards because of the cheapness of necessaries, both in Wiltshire and London. The justices of Wiltshire acted "having considered together with respect to the present times and the cheapness of all sortes of provisions (praised be God for the same) with due consideration of all other circumstances necessary to be considered of";[1] while the Carpenters' Company had been requested to advise the Lord Mayor of London in the matter of "the reducing of the excessive wages of Laborers and workemen in these times of great plenty".[2] Tawney suggests that this scaling-down may explain the "comparatively numerous assessments of the Restoration period".[3] Scaling-up again is indicated by the wording "more grievously charged than in times past" in a Warwickshire assessment of 1672;[4] but the phrase "having a special regard to the prices of provisions" in a 1738 rature for the same county is misleading, since the general increase in wages as compared with the scale of 1730 was not, in fact, accompanied by any substantial rise in prices.[5]

Information of this direct character being scanty, we have to fall back upon an attempt to decide whether there was any significant correlation between the justices' actions and the movement of prices. It is fairly clear, for instance, that the Chester authorities had changes in the cost-of-living particularly in mind when they reassessed wages in 1596 and the following year,[6] for a comparison of the yearly rates without meat and drink set in 1593, 1596 and 1597 shows an increase in each of the later years in all of the thirty-nine categories; while of the daily rates *with* meat

[1] *Wilts. C.R.*, 290.
[2] *E.J.* X, 406.
[3] *V.S.W.* XI, 330.
[4] Ashby, 171–2.
[5] *Ibid.* 175.
[6] I have not examined prices for Chester or district in these years, but the changes mentioned can hardly have any other explanation than that given, while a substantial increase in wheat prices between 1593 and 1596 is, for what it is worth in this connection, shown by Thorold Rogers' series (Rogers, *History* V, 268).

6

(compiled from data in *Somerset Q.S. Records* III and reissue

	1647	1648	1650	1651	1652	1653	1654
1. Menservants by the year		4 0 0	4 0 0	4 6 8	4 10 0	4 10 0	4 0 0
2. Maidservants by the year		2 0 0	2 0 0	2 0 0	2 0 0	2 0 0	1 13 4
HAY HARVEST							
3. Mowers per diem, finding themselves	1 4	1 4	1 4	1 6	1 8	1 8	1 4
4. Mowers per diem, at meat and drink	8	8	8	9	9	1 0	8
5. Men making hay, finding themselves	10	1 0	1 0	1 0	1 0	1 0	10
6. Men making hay, at meat and drink	6	6	6	6	6	6	4
7. Women making hay, finding themselves	8	8	8	8	8	8	5
8. Women making hay, at meat and drink	4	4	4	4	4	4	3
CORN HARVEST							
9. Men at corn harvest, finding themselves	1 4	1 2	1 2	1 4	1 4	1 4	1 2
10. Men at corn harvest, at meat and drink	8	8	8	8	8	8	6
11. Women at corn harvest, finding themselves	1 0	1 0	1 0	1 0	1 0	1 0	8
12. Women at corn harvest, at meat and drink	6	6	6	6	6	6	4
13. Masons, carpenters and tilers from 15 Mar. to 15 Sep. finding themselves				}1 2	}1 2	}1 2	}1 0
14. Masons, carpenters and tilers from 15 Sep. to 15 Mar. finding themselves							
15. Masons, carpenters and tilers from 15 Mar. to 15 Sep. at meat and drink				} 8	} 8	} 8	} 6
16. Masons, carpenters and tilers from 15 Sep. at meat and drink							
17. Threshers and ditchers from 15 Mar. to 15 Sep. finding themselves				}1 0	}1 0	}1 0	} 10
18. Threshers and ditchers from 15 Sep. to 15 Mar. finding themselves							
19. Threshers and ditchers from 15 Mar. to 15 Sep. at meat and drink				} 6	} 6	} 6	} 5
20. Threshers and ditchers from 15 Sep. to 15 Mar. at meat and drink							
PIECE WORK							
21. Mowing an acre of grass finding themselves							
22. Mowing an acre of grass to hay							
23. Mowing an acre of barley							
24. Cutting and binding an acre of wheat							
25. Mowing an acre of oats							
26. Cutting and binding an acre of beans							
27. Drawing an acre of hemp							

IV, by kind permission of the Somerset Record Society)

	1655	1666	1668	1669	1670 reissue	1671	1672	1673	1674 reissue	1675 reissue	1676	1677	1685
	4 0 0	4 0 0	4 0 0	4 0 0	4 0 0	4 0 0	4 0 0	4 0 0	4 0 0	4 0 0	4 0 0	4 0 0	4 10 0
	2 0 0	2 0 0	2 0 0	2 0 0	2 0 0	2 0 0	2 0 0	2 0 0	2 0 0	2 0 0	2 0 0	2 0 0	2 10 0
	1 4	1 4	1 4	1 4	1 4	1 4	1 4	1 2	1 2	1 2	1 2	1 2	1 2
	10	8	8	8	8	8	8	7	7	7	7	7	7
	10	1 0	1 0	1 0	1 0	10	10	10	10	10	10	10	10
	5	6	6	6	6	6	6	6	6	6	6	6	6
	-	-	-	-	-	-	-	-	-	-	-	-	7
	-	-	-	-	-	-	-	-	-	-	-	-	4
	1 0	1 4	1 2	1 2	1 2	1 4	1 2	1 0	1 0	1 0	1 0	-	1 2
	6	8	7	7	7	8	7	6	6	6	6	-	8
	10	10	10	10	10	10	10	9	9	9	7	7	-
	4	6	5	5	5	6	6	5	5	5	5	5	-
} 1 0		1 4	1 2	1 2	1 2	1 4	1 4	1 2	1 2	1 2	1 2	1 2	1 2
		1 2	1 0	-	-	-	1 2	1 0	1 0	1 0	1 0	1 0	1 0
} 6		8	7	6	6	6	8	7	7	7	7	7	7
		7	6	-	-	-	7	6	6	6	-	-	7
} 10		1 0	10	10	10	1 0	1 0	10	10	10	10	10	10
		10	9	9	9	10	10	8	8	8	8	8	8
} 5		6	5	5	5	6	6	5	5	5	5	5	5
		5	4	4	4	5	5	4	4	4	4	4	4
		1 2	1 2	1 4	1 4	-	1 2	1 2	1 2	1 2	1 2	1 2	1 2
		1 6	1 4	-	-	1 2	1 6	1 6	1 6	1 6	1 6	1 6	1 6
		10	10	10	10	-	10	10	10	10	10	10	1 1
		3 0	3 0	3 0	3 0	3 0	3 0	3 0	3 0	3 0	3 0	3 0	3 0
						10							
						2 0					2 0	2 0	2 0
											4 6		4 6

INDICES OF EXETER WHEAT ASSIZE PRICES
(Compiled from data kindly supplied by Sir William Beveridge)
Mean of 40 years 1640-79 taken as 100

1645	106	1655	105	1665	83	1675	73
1646	120	1656	106	1666	71	1676	73
1647	148	1657	113	1667	69	1677	102
1648	104	1658	103	1668	106	1678	93
1649	102	1659	107	1669	97	1679	75
1650	127	1660	120	1670	83	1680	76
1651	123	1661	138	1671	75	1681	96
1652	97	1662	100	1672	81	1682	90
1653	72	1663	93	1673	129	1683	86
1654	62	1664	87	1674	123	1684	85
						1685	59

and drink, thirty-six show a fall, nine remain stationary, and only one shows a rise, in the four-year period.[1] The series of Somerset assessments in the seventeenth century enables us to examine the action taken by the justices there rather more closely. If we take as a basis for roughly measuring price movements the mean of wheat assize prices in Exeter for the forty-year period 1640-79, the first assessment to be dealt with—that of 1647—was published (as can be seen from the table) at a time when prices were substantially above normal.[2] The following year's rature of 1648, claimed, as we have seen, to take into account high prices (they had been 48 per cent. above normal in the previous year). Despite the statement that rates for such as find themselves were raised, however, the only increase of this character was one of 2d. a day for men making hay. There was actually a corresponding *reduction*, moreover, for men at corn harvest finding themselves— harvest prospects were evidently good. These hopes were apparently justified, for prices that year were nearly back

[1] The assessments are printed in Morris, 367-8.
[2] As wages were assessed at Easter time, the prices for the *previous* harvest year will in each case be treated as those the justices had in mind.

to normal, and remained so in 1649. 1650, however, saw a substantial rise in the cost-of-living (wheat prices were 27 per cent. above normal) and in the 1651 rature some increases were sanctioned. Mowers finding themselves were to be allowed 2d. a day extra, as were men at corn harvest finding themselves. There seems, too, to have been a slight shortage of male labour, for menservants' yearly rates were raised from £4 to £4 6s. 8d., while the daily rate for mowers having meat and drink provided for them was raised by 1d. The cost-of-living remained high in 1651, and in the 1652 assessment mowers finding themselves were allotted a further 2d. a day. Labour, too, seems still to have been scarce—the increase for mowers with meat and drink was maintained, while wages for menservants on a yearly basis were increased by a further 3s. 4d. Prices fell to their normal level again in 1652, but no cut was made in the wages of those finding themselves, while a further increase of 3d. a day was sanctioned for mowers with meat and drink. As prices continued to fall—they were 28 per cent. below the mean in 1653—rates for those finding themselves were, however, brought back to the level of 1650 or earlier. Thus of workers finding themselves the daily rate for mowers was reduced 4d.; for men making hay 2d.; for women making hay 3d.; for women at corn harvest 4d. (the first reduction, incidentally, to take place in these last two categories); men at corn harvest 2d. Similar reductions were made in the case of masons, carpenters, tilers, threshers and ditchers. In addition, however, the shortage of labour had apparently subsided. Men servants' yearly rates were brought back to the 1650 level and maidservants were temporarily reduced from £2 to £1 13s. 4d. (this latter reduction only operated for one year, the rate being subsequently brought back to £2 and kept there). Daily workers with meat and drink were affected in the same way. The mowers' increases of 3d. and 1d. were cancelled, men and women making hay had their rates reduced by 2d. and 1d. respectively, men and women at corn harvest suffered reductions of 2d. each, masons and those in the categories following them in the list also had their wages with meat and drink reduced. Broadly speaking then, the 1654 assessment brought the rates of men finding themselves back to the 1647 level, while the rates of those at meat and drink, as well as those of women both finding themselves and at meat and drink, were reduced even below that level. In 1654 prices fell further. The only changes for those finding themselves in the assessment of 1655, however, were a reduction of 2d. for men at corn harvest and an *increase* of 2d. for women at corn harvest. The rates for mowers and men making hay at meat and drink were, however, increased by 2d. and 1d. respectively—evidently the cuts of the previous year had been too drastic, and difficulty was being experienced in obtaining labour.

An unfortunate gap in the sessions records deprives us of further information regarding the changes made in assessed rates until 1666. Though the assessment of that year followed two years of low prices—13 and 17 per cent. below the mean of 1664 and 1665 respectively—there were certain *increases* in rates for those finding themselves as compared with the 1655 position. Thus men making hay had an increase of 2d., men at corn harvest an increase of 4d. and masons and those in the categories following them also experienced increases. There were increases in the rates for those at meat and drink as well—men making hay, men at corn harvest, women at corn harvest and the artificers. Mowers at meat and drink, however, who had, as we have seen, been the first amongst the daily workers to reflect a labour scarcity in the fifties, had their rate reduced by 2d. Yearly rates for menservants and maidservants remained absolutely stable for this and the following years (the first change of which we know from the printed records being an increase in 1685). 1666 saw a further fall of prices, which was maintained in 1667. The assessment of 1668 made some reductions—2d. a day in the rates of those finding themselves and also reductions of 1d. a day in a number of rates including meat and drink. In

1668 prices recovered, and few changes were made in the 1669 assessment. This assessment was reissued unchanged in 1670, prices in 1669 being about average. There was a reduction in the cost-of-living in 1670, and in the 1671 assessment men making hay finding themselves were given 2d. a day less. At the same time, however, certain other categories of workers finding themselves actually had their rates increased—men at corn harvest by 2d., masons, carpenters and tilers by 2d., and threshers and ditchers by similar amounts. A temporary scarcity of labour seems to have been the real reason for these increases, however, for quite a number of categories "at meat and drink" show small increases also. There was a further fall of prices in 1671; and the 1672 assessment removed two of the increases of the previous year—men at corn harvest finding themselves had their increase of 2d. a day cancelled, as well as the 1d. a day increase for those not finding themselves. 1672 was another year of low prices, and the 1673 assessment, probably influenced by this and by a satisfactory labour market position, included reductions of 2d. and 1d. respectively for most categories of workers finding themselves and at meat and drink. There was a sharp rise in the cost-of-living in 1673, to 29 per cent. above normal, but the low scale of 1673 was reissued in 1674 without alteration. In January 1673-4 the Court had taken notice that badgers were enhancing prices and putting the poor to much trouble, and had ordered that no corn be bought in the market until the poor were served.[1] Peyton, commenting on this, observes that "from the bare text, it is difficult to reconcile the justices' concern for the poor, with the continuance of the low scale if the statute were strictly enforced".[2] This scale was, moreover, reissued in 1675, though 1674 prices were still 23 per cent. above the mean. Subsequent issues, with insignificant alterations, in 1676 and 1677 were, however, accompanied by a fall in prices in 1675 which was maintained in the following year. This is as

[1] *Somerset Q.S. Records* IV, 147.
[2] *Kesteven Q.S. Minutes*, p. cxii.

far as the volumes of printed sessions records take us, but one further rature, for 1685, has been printed. It shows remarkably few alterations as compared with the last assessments we have considered. Men at corn harvest, however, had their rates increased, as did both yearly menservants and maidservants.

What does this Somerset evidence, to which perhaps more attention than is justified has been given, suggest? It would appear, in the first place, that even here, where the justices, unlike those in most districts, were prepared to alter the scale at frequent intervals, the cost-of-living aspect was subordinate to the factor of labour scarcity. Particularly in the later part of the period covered by these ratures it will have been noticed how frequently changes in the rates of those finding themselves, which might at first sight have been taken to represent changes in living costs, are accompanied by corresponding changes in the rates for those at meat and drink. A second and closely related conclusion which may be put forward is that the justices were more often in this series attempting adjustments between different categories of worker than applying flat-rate increases or decreases throughout the scale. Both these conclusions, incidentally, contrast strongly with the Chester situation in the fifteen-nineties when, as we have seen, rates even for the widely different crafts covered by the assessments, tended to be altered *en bloc*. The first of these conclusions is, it will be noticed, in line with Tawney's experience, for though he found a rough parallelism in the rise of wheat prices and wages in one or two instances, he more often found there seemed to be no correspondence at all. Two factors which he advanced to explain this were the need for a "differential" to ensure a supply of agricultural labour, and the circumstance that the justices themselves belonged to a class which felt a rise in prices severely, as their copyhold and freehold tenants' rents were fixed.[1] I cannot altogether agree, however, with another conclusion of Tawney's when he says that "if movements in wages had been ad-

[1] *V.S.W.* XI, 558–60.

justed with any accuracy to movements in prices, it would have been necessary for them to take place not only from year to year, but from month to month, and, indeed, almost from day to day".[1] The Somerset material we have just examined seems to me to suggest, not so much that it was impossible for a year-to-year adjustment to cost-of-living changes to be achieved, as that, although this was done on occasion, the factor of labour scarcity had also to be taken into account and tended increasingly to become the dominant consideration. It is admitted, of course, that for such an adjustment frequent alteration in the scale, as was actually done in Somerset, was necessary; and that where the practice of reissue without alteration, except when factors of major importance supervened, obtained, the attempt had obviously been abandoned. To admit that the justices were not as a rule prepared to take the trouble, however, or that they did not wish to secure this yearly adjustment, is not to admit that it could not have been achieved if desired, particularly as the central authority obviously thought of the annual nature of assessment as making it possible to provide just such an adjustment. The regulation of markets and the fixing of prices of food supplies was, it is true, a policy which the central government invariably brought to the attention of local authorities at times of scarcity. That this latter policy was regarded by the Council as making the annual adjustment of wages to changes in the cost-of-living unnecessary, however, is not, I think, proved. The evidence would seem to suggest that the two were regarded as complementary—after all, the smaller the proportion of people coming wholly within the categories in wage assessments, the more necessary regulation of markets and of grain supplies and prices obviously was. If the justices tended to prefer the latter policy to the former, it was no doubt because it was in their interests to do so, rather than because the machinery of wage assessment was totally unfitted for one of the purposes for which it had been, ostensibly at least, devised.

[1] *V.S.W.* XI, 337.

For the same reasons, I cannot subscribe to one of the propositions advanced by Miss Hindmarsh in this connection. Her contention is that assessments were never intended for those entirely dependent upon their wages, but for a population which was hardly affected by fluctuations in the prices of food.[1] While freely admitting that, in point of numbers, the class of landless labourers was not a large one, and had to be augmented as a labour force by those with land, it seems to me that the modification of assessed rates to meet increases in the cost-of-living was intended, *inter alia*, to dissuade this landless class from adopting the alternative policy of leaving work and squatting on the waste.[2] In this sense employers of agricultural labour who increasingly gave wages with board or with allowances in kind, and the central government recommending the revision of official scales in times of high prices, were tackling the same problem in slightly different ways—if the former expedient appealed to employers more than the latter, this constitutes no proof that the rating of wages was not devised partly to meet such a situation or that it could not, given the co-operation of those charged with its execution, have succeeded. Moreover, a clear distinction could not always be drawn between changes in the cost-of-living incidental to monetary factors (which the Act was surely intended to provide for) and those arising from other factors.

There remain to be considered additional means whereby pressure was, at different times, brought to bear on the justices to alter or enforce the assessed rates so that wage-earners might be able to obtain a living. So far in this study we have spoken of the Statute of Artificers as providing for the assessment of *maximum* rates. There is evidence, however, that the justices sometimes regarded them as *minimum* rates, a point mentioned in a previous chapter in connection with compelling masters to pay wages due. At a Holland sessions in 1667, for instance, a certain John Brassey was indicted for refusing to pay John Clark, firstly for hay-

[1]Hindmarsh, 147.
[2]See note at the end of this chapter.

making and secondly for diking, *according to the assessed rates*.[1] Miss Hindmarsh records that in 1625 the Sussex justices circumvented an attempt on the part of the King's Purveyors to pay workers in that county less than the assessed rates,[2] though in this case it seems to me possible that all that was involved was an undertaking to pay the rates current in the district—an obligation not necessarily applying to *other* employers. Again, a 1724 Nottinghamshire wage assessment contains the phrase "where less wages have been given than are hereby appointed within one year past, that such less wages shall be given and taken still",[3] the implication being that, but for this permission, the assessed rates would have been treated as legal minima; while a Warwickshire assessment of 1657 declares that the rates "shall be such and no more".[4] Moreover, there are occasional passages in the textbooks used by justices which would have supported their adopting an attitude of this kind. There is such a passage in Burn's *Justice of the Peace*—"in order to intitle the servant to wages he needed not to prove how much his master had agreed to pay him, *for that was fixed by the justices*,[5] but only how long he had served, and then the wages followed of course".[6] Dalton, more reasonably, seems to apply such reasoning only to cases where master and servant had not mentioned the matter of wages. "If a man retaineth a laborer or servant, to serve him according to the Statute, though no wages be spoken of upon the retainer, yet the retainer is good, and they shall have such wages as are assessed and appointed by Proclamation, for that wages are certain".[7] It is interesting to note, also, a case in which, in certain circumstances, local opinion seems to have compelled the payment of the statutory rates as

[1]Holland Q.S. Minutes, Mich. 1677.
[2]Hindmarsh, 142.
[3]Copnall, 65.
[4]Ashby, 170; similar wording is found in a few other assessments.
[5]My italics.
[6]Burn, 626.
[7]Dalton, 127. This probably explains the Kent justices' procedure, *E.H.R.* XLIII, 401.

minima. Amongst the customs of the township of Weeton,
East Yorkshire, put into writing in November 1669, the
third contains a clause to the effect that if certain fences
are out of repair the byelawmen shall give twenty-four
hours notice to the owners or occupiers concerned and,
should the latter not put matters right, shall set workmen
to make the fence right, and if the owners or occupiers
"refuse to pay within 24 houres after the work be Dun such
wages for such work as ye statute will allow then it shall be
lawfull to distreine praise and sell . . . deducting reasonable
charges".[1] When these customs were again committed to
writing in 1714, this particular one was repeated. In a
loose way, of course, the desire expressed in the Statute to
afford the hired person both in time of scarcity and in time
of plenty a "convenient proportion" of wages[2] might be
taken as implying the idea of wages not falling below a
standard, and letters from the Privy Council (as, for
instance, the one quoted later in this chapter)[3] sometimes
use wording of the same type. As is well known, however,
the only definite statutory justification for treating the
justices' rates as minima was restricted to the clothing
industries—"if any clothier or other . . . shall not pay so
much or so great wages to their weavers, spinsters, workmen
or workwomen as shall be so . . . rated . . . every clothier . . .
so offending shall forfeit and lose for every such offence,
to the party aggrieved, ten shillings;" and clothiers who
happened to be justices were not to take part in the assessment of wages for clothing workers.[4] Not only the State
but also the town authorities tended to apply a minimum
to this industry,[5] probably because the early emergence of
clothiers as entrepreneurs necessitated action of this kind.[6]

As to the extent to which the justices carried out their
statutory obligations in this matter, we know that in June

[1]Welwick Byelawmen's and Miscellaneous Accounts Book.
[2]5 Eliz. c. 4.
[3]Post, 81–2.
[4]1 Jac. I, c. 6.
[5]V.S.W. XI, 315–6.
[6]Ibid. XI, 544–5.

1614, as a result of a petition from the poor craftsmen of Wiltshire, a letter was sent from the Privy Council to the justices there which included the following paragraph. "And whereas it is understood that many of those poore craftsmen are for the most parte weavers and belonging unto the mistery of cloathing, and doe cheifely complaine on the small wadges gyven them by the clothier, being no more then what was accustomed to be payde 40 yeres past, notwithstanding that the prises of all kinde of victuall are almost doubled from what they were, it is also thought fitting that, having called the clothiers before you, you examine the truthe of this complaint, and finding it to be as is informed, to use your best endevors for the proportioning of their wadges unto the state of these present tymes, as in all other trades it is observed".[1] The earlier part of this letter had ordered the justices to restrain maltsters, millers, badgers and drivers who enhanced the market, or to diminish their number. At the summer sessions that year the justices duly took steps of this latter type;[2] but whether they did anything in the matter of the wages paid by clothiers we cannot, from what has been printed, say. In 1623, however, the weavers and spinners petitioned the justices, asking them "to appoint certain grave and discreete persons to view the straitnes of workes, to assease rates for wages according to the desert of their workes, now especially in this great dearth of corne."[3] The justices accordingly ordered the workers and employers concerned "to be at the Devizes the Thursday in the next Whitson weeke, to conferr with us hereabouts".[4] The order resulting from that meeting was to the effect that the general table of wages should continue as formerly assessed, and that the wages fixed for those connected with clothing should be published on the next market day "in order that workmasters and workmen alike may take notice thereof, and that the workmen who

[1] *Acts of the Privy Council 1613–14*, 458.
[2] *H.M.C. Various* I, 87.
[3] *Ibid.* 94: Bland, 356–7.
[4] *Ibid.*

desire that the same rates may stand may be the better satisfied".[1] Apparently, therefore, the workers' request for a re-assessment of wages was not met, the existing rates being proclaimed afresh.

In the years 1629-31 the Council, as those concerned with the history of poor relief have noticed, seems to have been particularly active in this matter. To begin with, in 1629 the Essex authorities were told that the weavers of baize in the Bocking and Braintree district should be remunerated on a just and reasonable basis.[2] In February of the following year the textile workers of Sudbury petitioned that their wages had been abated, notwithstanding the present state of scarcity and dearth.[3] Commissioners were accordingly appointed to inquire into the matter and, as a result of their investigations, the Essex justices made a special order setting forth the piece-rates that the saymakers of Sudbury were to pay.[4] This particular matter does not, however, seem to have been satisfactorily adjusted until some years later.[5] In the meantime, the Council had, in September 1630, sent letters to Cambridge, Essex, Suffolk, Norfolk and Norwich, pointing out that the hard and necessitous times being experienced formed a clear case for the putting into execution of the Statutes 5 Elizabeth c. 4, and 1 James I c. 6, so that "the poore should not be pinched in theise times of scarcitie and dearth".[6] (The Suffolk justices had already, apparently without previous pressure of this kind, re-assessed wages the previous April).[7] It has not, of course, escaped notice that it was to the cloth-working districts that these letters were sent.[8] For other

[1]*H.M.C Various* I, 94.
[2]Leonard, 160.
[3]Bland, 358.
[4]*Ibid*, 359–60.
[5]Leonard, 161.
[6]*E.H.R.* XIII, 91.
[7]*E.H.R.* XII, 307–11. The statement in Hampson, 48, that "the towns of Bury St. Edmunds and Norwich, which had received similar communications from the Council, definitely did draw up new assessments as a consequence" apparently overlooks this difference in dates.
[8]*V.S.W.* XI, 552–3.

counties a more general letter, dated June 1630 and sent to all cities and counties, detailing measures to be taken to keep down the price and maintain the supply of bread and grain for poor people, was deemed sufficient.[1] Wage assessment as a means of alleviating hardship in an emergency of this kind was, apparently, thought of by the Council as mainly applicable to clothworking counties.

It is by no means certain that appropriate action was taken by the justices on receipt of the letter reminding them of the Acts of 1562-3 and 1603-4. A report of the justices of some of the Cambridgeshire hundreds in 1632 (which was not, however, intended as a reply to this particular letter) included the statement that they had taken the Statute and questions relating to retaining of servants and ordering of wages into their consideration, "but have perfected nothinge, the care of the poore and puttinge forth of apprentices hath imployed soe much of our tyme".[2] The reply of the Norwich justices, in December 1630, seems at first sight, it is true, to be favourable, and has been generally accepted as meaning that a new assessment was drawn up. "And we have accordinge to the Statute appointed the wages of servants, laborers and workemen at such Rates as will conveniently recompence their paynes and yeld unto them competent maintenaunce".[3] This could, however, merely mean that the old rates, which the justices considered to be still adequate, had been confirmed, and a close examination of the Norwich records rather suggests that the latter interpretation is the correct one. For not only is there no hint in the Court records of a new assessment having been drawn up at this time (and both the Quarter Sessions and the Mayor's Court Books normally refer to this particular question); but there is definite record of wages being continued on 10th August 1629, and again continued in 5 Charles 1, the day and month being, unfortunately,

[1] This letter (Privy Council Register, 13th June 1630) was, of course, later supplemented by a Book of Orders (Privy Council Register, 9th September 1630).
[2] Hampson, 48.
[3] Leonard, 163.

eaten away.[1] Furthermore it is significant that their letter of December 1630 to the Council was intended mainly as an answer to the latter's general letter dated 13th June; this is made perfectly clear by the entries in the Norwich Court records in connection with the reply—no mention is made of the inclusion of any reference to wages, which looks very much as if it was an afterthought. However, justices of certain counties which did not, to our knowledge, receive special instructions in the matter,[2] took steps which must, one would think, have represented an attempt to bring the assessed rates into line with the sharp rise in the cost-of-living. Thus the justices of at least two divisions of Hertfordshire drew up an assessment in 1631,[3] which included a section for clothing workers. Spinsters' and weavers' piece-rates, it may be mentioned, were, unlike any other piece-rates in the assessment, given without the qualifying phrase "not above"; while the yearly rates for weavers' servants were distinguished from other yearly rates in the same way. (Incidentally in the Suffolk assessment of 1630, where similar rates appear together, the qualification "not above" is also omitted in the sections on husbandry, probably due to carelessness).[4] Again, the Gloucester[5] and Herefordshire[6] justices drew up new assessments in 1632. Finally, amongst the justices' reports on the execution of the 1631 Book of Orders (which was, of course, more concerned with other statutes, but naturally referred to the "poor law" aspects of 5 Elizabeth c. 4)[7] there was one from the Mayor of Guildford which spoke of causing the Statute of Labourers to be put in execution,[8] one from certain Cambridgeshire hundreds (which we have noticed already),[9] and one from the

---

[1]Norwich Court Records. The illegible entry is on a page which has been rebound, so that its position provides no clue as to the month.

[2]Beyond the references to 5 Eliz. c. 4 in the Book of Orders 1631.

[3]See Appendix I.

[4]E.H.R. XII, 307–11.

[5]Rogers, *History* VI, 694.

[6]H.M.C. *Portland* III, 31.

[7]Leonard, 343.

[8]*Ibid*, 358.

[9]*Ante*, 83.

justices of a Derbyshire wapentake reporting "that the
Statute for Labourers and for the ordering of wages was
carried out, and that none were presented to them for refusing to work at reasonable wages".[1]

When this Privy Council supervision—which Tawney
ascribes in part to "a desire to prevent agitation by removing the material causes of discontent, and incidentally to
put pressure on the middle and upper classes, who were
the stronghold of religious and constitutional opposition"[2]—
was relaxed, it was not to be expected that the justices would
constantly keep the cost-of-living aspect of wage regulation
in mind. There continued to be a significant absence of
cases, in Quarter Sessions records, of clothiers being accused
of not paying the assessed rates.[3] The later Hertfordshire
assessments[4] omit any mention of piece-rates for clothworkers;[5] while the 1647 West Riding assessment treats
clothworkers on the same basis as other workers—they shall
not take for their wages above so much per day or per
year[6]—and, from 1671 onwards, the West Riding justices
apparently ceased to assess wages for such workers altogether.[7] The Devonshire justices, while continuing to
include rates for spinners in their assessments, renewed the
1679 rates without change up to 1790.[8] We are probably
justified in concluding that, by 1640,[9] the attempt to provide a minimum for clothworkers was at an end, the
Gloucestershire dispute of 1756-7[10] merely serving to show
that, though the existing law was on the side of the workers,
the arguments used by the clothiers had a stronger appeal

[1]*V.C.H. Derbyshire* II, 182.
[2]*V.S.W.* XI, 552-3.
[3]If we ignore presentments such as the following—"all clothiers
and serge makers who do put work to any spinsters by the bundle or
any other term than the just pound of 16 ounces" (*Somerset Q.S.
Records* IV, 224).
[4]*Hertford C.R.* I, 292: VI, 400.
[5]They give yearly rates for journeymen, however.
[6]*E.J.* XXIV, 223-5.
[7]*Ibid.* 228-9.
[8]Hoskins, 130.
[9]*V.S.W.* XI, 332.
[10]Fully dealt with in Lipson III, 266-70.

7

to the legislature. One cannot be equally definite about it, but the evidence strongly suggests that, from the latter part of the seventeenth century, the cost-of-living ceased to be a major consideration in assessment.[1] Henceforth the emphasis was on another aspect of wage regulation, to be discussed in the following chapter.

Note: In support of the argument advanced on page 78, it may be pointed out that the framers of the 1563 policy were, in one respect, merely returning to the practice laid down in a Statute of 1389-90[2]—the non-employment of the "statutory limit" arrangement in force before and after the latter date was deliberate, and must surely have been due as much as anything else to a desire to give *local* conditions (both in respect of food and labour scarcity) greater weight.

---

[1]The general trend of prices was, it is true, downward for some time thereafter; but there were individual years of scarcity which would have justified changes in assessments.

[2]*Econ. H. R.* I, 138.

CHAPTER VI

THE "EXCESSIVE EXACTIONS" ASPECT

ONE of the first things likely to strike anyone about the wage assessment provision of the Statute of Artificers was that, providing as it did for a legal maximum wage, it was not in the interests of the wage-earner. Previous legislation of this type had been intended, in part, to keep wages down, while Cecil's preliminary draft of the Bill alluded to the unreasonable wages demanded by servants in husbandry.[1] Not unnaturally, therefore, Thorold Rogers looked with suspicion on the claim made in the Act that it was intended to ensure a convenient proportion of wages both in plenty and in scarcity. "I contend that from 1563 to 1824," he declared, "a conspiracy . . . was entered into to cheat the English workman of his wages, to tie him to the soil, to deprive him of hope, and to degrade him into irremediable poverty."[2] Other writers of the same period came, after examination of Quarter Sessions material, to the same conclusion. Cox, for instance, speaks of "this odious Act . . . the results of which were so momentous and delivered English labour, tied and bound, into the hands of the most interested capitalists for nearly three centuries".[3] Even those who saw good in the Statute could not deny that it had potentialities of this character. Stress could, of course, be laid—as, for instance, by Cunningham[4]—on the significance of the amending Act providing a minimum for clothworkers; but, as we have seen, both the application

[1] *V.S.W.* XI, 323-4.
[2] Rogers, *Six Centuries*, 398.
[3] Cox II, 237.
[4] *E.J.* IV, 515.

of this minimum and emphasis on the cost-of-living in assessment depended on a considerable measure of central supervision. There remained, it is true, the faint possibility that the grave and discreet persons whose advice was, by the terms of the Statute,[1] to be obtained, might have the interests of artificers and labourers and servants at heart. Where, as happened in a few counties, the Grand Jury presented their opinion as to the rates they thought suitable, the cost-of-living aspect might occasionally be stressed— this happened, for instance, in Somerset in 1647-50,[2] while the Essex Grand Jury recommended increases in 1599 and 1611;[3] from what we know of the composition of such juries, however, it is not surprising to find one in Worcestershire making the following presentment, which has caught the attention of most writers on the subject—"we desire that servants' wages may be rated according to the Statute, for we find the unreasonableness of servants' wages a great grievance so that servants are grown [so] proud and idle [that the master cannot be known from the servant, except it be because the servant wears better clothes than his master]".[4] It seems probable that, where advice was taken at all, the Grand Jury was used for this purpose;[5] it is just possible, however, that the time at which the committee of justices charged with the rating of wages in the East Riding was directed to meet—six o'clock in the evening— may indicate that some attempt was made to choose a time convenient for the appearance of wage-receivers whose advice might be asked, particularly as the times of meeting of other committees seem almost invariably to have been earlier in the day than this.[6] On at least one occasion the London magistrates sought the advice of the Carpenters' Company, the latter co-operating with them "for the reduc-

[1] 5 Eliz. c. 4, sec. 11.
[2] *Somerset Q.S. Records* III, 40, 67, 121.
[3] Hindmarsh, 49.
[4] *H.M.C. Various* I, 322: Bland, 361. The portions in square brackets were crossed out in the original.
[5] In addition to the cases mentioned, this is also true of Staffordshire (Staffs. Sessions Books, April 1656).
[6] East Riding Order Books, Easter 1722.

ing of the excessive wages of laborers and workmen in these times of great plenty";[1] and the Lindsey justices may possibly have taken the advice of the chief constables—"the rates of wages to continue for the year following confirmed under the hands of the Chief Constables".[2] What little evidence we have on the question of advice taken does not, therefore, materially alter the position. Moreover when, after the Great Fire of London, it was desired to prevent workmen taking advantage of the demand for building labour to force up its price, (or, as the Act put it, making "the common Calamity a Pretence to extort unreasonable ... wages") the assessment of wages was the method chosen; the Act of 1666[3] was for the express purpose of preventing "excessive exactions".

The assessment of wages, then, had as one of its purposes that of keeping wages below the level they would otherwise have reached, of preventing the exploitation of a labour scarcity situation by those who stood to benefit by it, of maintaining the traditional and therefore natural rate of wages as against what laisser-faire economists later came to describe as the "natural" rate. It will be clear from what has been said earlier that wage assessment was only one among a number of expedients which, separately or in conjunction according to circumstances, could be employed for this purpose. Of these expedients, proceedings against those living idly or at their own hands, or refusing to work for reasonable wages, were naturally often used instead of (or along with) wage assessment to combat the excessive exactions of workers. Thus a West Riding order of 1641 mentioned "a general complaint of the inhabitants of these parts that servants refuse to work for reasonable wages, and cannot be hired for competent allowance as formerly, making advantage of the much business of the times";[4] while a well-known Wiltshire order of 1655 aptly illustrates the close relationship between assessment and other parts

[1]*E.J.* X, 406.
[2]Lindsey Q.S. Minutes, April 1666.
[3]19 Charles II, c. 3.
[4]*W.R.S. Records 1611–42*, 333.

of the policy. The assessed rates had duly been proclaimed "but young people both men and maids, fitting for service, will not go abroad to service without they may have excessive wages, but will rather work at home at their own hands, whereby the rating of wages will take little effect; therefore no young men or maids fitting to go abroad to service (their parents not being of ability to keep them) shall remain at home, but shall with all convenient speed betake themselves to service for the wages aforesaid, which if they refuse to do the justices shall proceed against them".[1] Refusing to go to service, and living at one's own hands must, indeed, as Tawney has suggested, often have been used as a lever for raising wages;[2] a further means to the same end was, as he points out, provided by the existence of waste land[3] which in this respect had much the same effect as did, at a later date, the American frontier, in its influence on the wages of those who did not migrate. Another weapon available to the worker—for preventing the use of which the Statute, as we have seen, did not fail to provide—was that of leaving before term, or before a piece of work was finished. The Council might upbraid justices who failed to assess wages in times of scarcity, but was itself quite capable of condemning attempts of labourers to exploit a scarcity situation—"we are informed that it is a thing usuall amongst workmen employed in such labours to exact great prises and high rates, when the worke growes to any perfeccion or finishing, then either take their owne unreasonable demandes, or to desert the worke, and so put the work maister to some extraordinaries".[4] Much the same complaint is made by the Hertfordshire justices in assessing wages in 1687. "Whereas the licentious humours of some servants have prevailed so far upon the Lenity and good nature of their masters, that they have advanced the charge of their wages and the expence of their diet above the rents of their Master's farms; and to highten this grievance they

[1] *H.M.C. Various* I, 132: Bland, 360.
[2] *V.S.W.* XI, 540.
[3] *Ibid.* 540–1.
[4] *Acts of the Privy Council, 1625–6*, 27–8.

have been soe exorbitant in their severall services, that they
will not work but at such times, and in such manner as they
please; and when their work is most necessary, they often-
times leave the same, if not their services".[1]   Another
"unreasonable and unlawful doing" is hinted at on the
same occasion for, in the list of offences and penalties
attached to the assessment, the ten-pound fine for con-
spiring together to advance wages is included.[2] We have
already noticed that a petition of householders and other
substantial persons presented to the Holland justices gave
as the reason for the holding of petty sessions only once a
year the reduction of the exorbitant demands of servants,
and suggested a return to the older practice of holding more
frequent statute sessions because the "one session" arrangement had served to enhance the rates and wages of servants,
who had tended to become more scarce since that procedure was put in operation; the justices, by complying with
this request, clearly indicated that they were in sympathy
with the attitude of these petitioners.[3]

It would, of course, be wrong to suppose that the justices
invariably reacted to a labour scarcity situation by enforcing the assessed rates that had previously obtained, and
compelling those living at home or at their own hands to
go to service. Sometimes they merely raised the assessed
rates and, so far as we know, took no special measures by
way of compulsion—this, at least, is suggested by a comparison of the Warwickshire assessments of 1730 and 1738.[4]
Sometimes the county justices, interested in maintaining
the supply of agricultural, as distinct from other labour,
sought to achieve this by advances in the assessed rates for
agricultural work, accompanied by no change, or a decline,
in the assessed rates for other categories. This, in Tawney's
opinion, was happening in Wiltshire in 1635 and in Warwickshire in 1672.[5] Sometimes labour would be accepted

[1]*Hertford C.R.* VI, 405.
[2]*Ibid.* VI, 406.
[3]Holland Q.S. Minutes, Easter 1726 (Kirton).
[4]Ashby, 175.
[5]*V.S.W.* XI, 560.

from other districts without insistence on a "settlement certificate" by way of indemnification against chargeability. Thus Chambers points out that in the printed records of Nottingham for the period 1700-60 there is not a single allusion to the settlement system, suggesting deliberate relaxation of the normal requirements of the time on entry.[1] Such a relaxation was, indeed, expressly provided for by the Somerset justices on one occasion.[2] "The Court declares that healthy single persons may go to any place to serve for one year, upon any legal retainer, such masters . . . (being payers to poor rates and other usual taxes) as are qualified in the judgment of the nearest justice to receive them: without any discharges being given to indemnify any parish to which they shall go from being chargeable by reason of their settling in service there".[3]

No doubt it would be equally wrong to assume too readily that the rating of wages, coupled with the enforcement of the assessed rates and compelling the idle to work, always signified a labour shortage. Cunningham suggested, for instance, that the Shropshire justices, faced with an unemployment problem, in 1732 assessed rates of wages at which men might be compelled to work,[4] (though this interpretation is not altogether satisfactory). Nevertheless, sufficient evidence exists to show that, faced with a labour shortage, the justices quite often took action on these lines. Thus Miss Hampson shows how the severe scarcity of agricultural labour in parts of Cambridgeshire was reflected by the activity of the County magistrates during the Restoration period in such matters as compelling the idle to work, enforcing public hiring, and insisting on testimonials.[5] Again, there is the case of Suffolk in the seventeen-twenties. In April 1723 an order was issued to the high constables requiring them to issue out their warrants to the overseers to bring in lists "of the several persons of the meaner sort

[1]Chambers, 271.
[2]1676.
[3]*Somerset Q.S. Records* IV, 190–1.
[4]*E.J.* IV, 514.
[5]Hampson, 54–7.

with the names and ages of their respective children that
the justices may judge who are fit to be bound out apprentices and who to go to service".[1] Both in this and the
following year numerous cases of living idly appear in the
Ipswich records; while in 1724—for the first time, judging
by the silence of minute and order books, for over half a
century—a Suffolk wage assessment was drawn up.[2] There
is evidence, too, that efforts were made to enforce it. For in
a little note-book drawn up just about this time, marked
"Precedents and Indictments", where samples of what
appear to be actual cases are given (presumably as a guide),
there is an instance of a master overpaying his servant,
whom he had hired outside statute sessions;[3] even if this
case were imaginary—which, in view of the names and
details given, seems unlikely—it still provides evidence that
the question of overpayment was liable to arise at this time,
for the number of types illustrated in the book is not large.
A final example—that of the justices of East and North
Yorkshire in the early sixteen-eighties—deserves rather
fuller treatment because it is possible to reconstruct the
whole episode fairly satisfactorily. The justices were, in
effect, faced with a temporary shortage of labour as a result
of an epidemic.

The least interesting aspect of the situation—the evidence
regarding the existence of an epidemic likely to bring about
a temporary scarcity of labour—can be summarized quite
shortly. According to my original plan in this case, a fairly
extensive sample of parishes in the area under review was
taken, and the recorded burials in the three years 1679-81
were compared with the mean of six years (the three pre-
ceding and the three following). Although this method
suggested that an epidemic affecting most of East and North
Yorkshire must have taken place at this time, it was open
to the objection that the years chosen for comparison might
not be representative—that the number of deaths in this

[1]Suffolk Order Books.
[2]Ibid. Easter 1727 (Beccles).
[3]Book of Precedents and Indictments, 89.

six-year period might be below normal. In order to meet this objection, fuller information was obtained about a smaller sample. Twenty-four of the parishes in the original sample provided burial figures for the whole of the thirty-year period 1664-1693. Taking these twenty-four as a new sample, it was found that in twenty-one of them the number of recorded burials in 1679 and 1680 was the largest for the thirty-year period. In the remaining three parishes, 1682 was the year with the highest number of recorded burials, 1680 being the second highest. Taking this sample as a whole, the highest years of twenty-one parishes and the second highest of three parishes exceeded the mean of the thirty years by 121 per cent. It can hardly be doubted that such a situation would, in a large agricultural area, be likely to lead to a temporary shortage of yearly farm servants, particularly as, in most of the parishes examined, several years of high mortality followed one another. So far as the epidemic is concerned, it is true that evidence other than that of parish registers is lacking; but Creighton, on the basis of contemporary London material, records an influenza in 1679, and epidemic agues extending over three seasons 1678-80.[1]

What policy did the justices adopt? Taking the East Riding first, although unfortunately both rolls and minutes are missing for the period under review, something can be learnt from two recently-discovered wage assessments; as these have already been printed, it will be sufficient to indicate their bearing on this particular inquiry.[2] The assessments are for 1669 and 1679 respectively, and while the first relates to the whole of the Riding, the second would appear to apply merely to the Ouse and Derwent Division. The first relevant point seems to be that the later assessment is prefaced, in the petty constable's memoranda book where it was found, by a set of rules summarizing the duties of masters, servants and constables as contained in the Statute of Artificers. We are, perhaps, justified in assuming

[1]Creighton, 328–35.
[2]E.H.R. LII, 283–9.

that it was not an accident that these rules should accompany the second rather than the first assessment; for if the justices proposed to attempt wage regulation under rather abnormal circumstances, it would be natural to provide a "refresher course" for those to whom unfamiliar duties would fall. A second point of interest is that the 1679 rature contains yearly wages only. This fits in very well with the circumstance (to which attention will be drawn in a moment) that all the North Riding presentments for overpayment were in connection with yearly wages. It would have been foolish to disturb the existing daily- and piece-rates for farm work and village crafts because of a temporary labour shortage; such a shortage would naturally show itself first in the hiring of yearly servants where, in any case, latitude had always to be allowed for differences in experience and efficiency. Corroboration of the nature of the situation with which the justices had to deal is, it may be suggested, provided by the absence of daily- and piece-rates in the 1679 assessment. A third point of significance is that the increases sanctioned were for yearly rates *with board*. These increases, as compared with the rates drawn-up ten years previously, ranged from twenty to sixty-seven per cent., the mean increase being thirty-six per cent.[1] As these changes in rates include board, they cannot well have been necessitated by a rise in the cost-of-living. There is, moreover, no reason to suppose that any substantial change in the demand for labour took place in these ten years. A change in the supply curve of labour, connected with factors other than the cost-of-living, would provide a reason; and the only factor likely to lead to such a change in this area at this time is, it would seem, increased mortality due to sickness.[2]

[1]Due to an unfortunate arithmetical slip, these three percentages were wrongly given in *E.H.R.* LII, 287; they are the only percentages affected by this slip, however.

[2]Concerted action by workers to raise wages would, quite apart from the legal obstacles involved, be unlikely in a large agricultural area; while migration on the necessary scale would have created problems elsewhere of which we should expect to have heard.

Our information regarding action taken by the North Riding justices is, of course, fuller. Action was first taken on 20th April 1680, when a new wage assessment for the whole of the Riding was drawn up; at the same time chief constables were ordered for the future to keep their statute sessions according to law, to inquire into offences against the Elizabethan labour code, and present them at the next sessions.[1] At the sessions held the following July, further steps were taken. The chief constables of the Western Division of the Riding were ordered to issue out their warrants to the petty constables requiring them to make their returns in writing, at the next statute sessions, of the usual details regarding masters and servants in their parishes (names, wages, and when contracts of service would terminate) as well as the names of masters and servants refusing to furnish the information required.[2] At the next sessions (in October) a similar order, relating to chief constables in the *Eastern* Division of the Riding, was made; and warrants were to be issued out against petty constables in the Western Division who had made imperfect returns, or had failed to make returns.[3] Then, in the following January, we find the first results of all this activity—presentments, evidently arising from the statute sessions of the previous Martinmas. One of these relates to an employer receiving a servant who had departed from her former master without permission.[4] The other relevant presentments relate to masters and servants agreeing to wages above the rates assessed the previous Easter. The way in which these presentments are recorded in the minutes, quite apart from their number, is of some interest.[5] Instead of merely stating that the following presentments were concerned with paying and receiving more than the allowed rates, as in previous instances in these minutes, and in similar instances elsewhere, the more elaborate method is

[1] *N.R.Q.S.R.* VII, 34.
[2] *Ibid.* VII, 38.
[3] *Ibid.* VII, 41.
[4] *Ibid.* VII, 44.
[5] *Ibid.* VII, 45.

adopted of giving one case in detail, and then adding a list giving the status and parish of other masters offending in this way, possibly to add emphasis or make the nature of the offence clearer. Thus we are told that twenty-six masters overpaid their maidservants, and twenty-seven their menservants in husbandry, and in one instance in each class the exact extent of the overpayment is noted.

There was an adjournment to Bedale a few days later, when five further presentments relating to overpayment of servants are recorded.[1] The justices evidently felt, however, that they must not confine their attention solely to raising the assessed rates and preventing these new rates from being exceeded; but that something should also be done to render the shortage itself less acute. When reminding the chief constables of the Western Division of their previous instructions, they therefore took the opportunity of ordering them also to issue out their warrants to the petty constables to make returns of all servants who, though able to work, remained at home, so that such action might be taken by the justices as the law directed.[2] The following Easter there were seven further presentments in which overpayment was the offence; the degree of overpayment, if we are to judge by the "sample" case given on each occasion, was steadily falling, however, either owing to an improvement in the labour position, or to the increasing success of the justices' policy. At subsequent sessions, indeed, nothing is heard of overpayment, though in July the petty constables of the Western Division are once more exhorted to deliver returns at the next statute sessions of all the names and ages of men and women servants remaining at home and not going to service.[3] By the following year the labour shortage has evidently ceased to be acute, for we find two presentments involving dismissal without legal cause.[4] It may be assumed that, apart altogether from a reduction

[1] N.R.Q.S.R. VII, 47.
[2] Ibid. VII, 48.
[3] Ibid. VII, 51.
[4] Ibid. VII, 54, 56.

of deaths, migration of farm labour into the North Riding had taken place, in response to higher wages, from adjacent districts not so seriously affected, and was by this time making itself felt.

At no point, it may be observed, is it expressly stated in the minutes that a labour shortage existed—the announcement that wages have been reassessed is not accompanied by any explanation of this action, and the subsequent orders and presentments we have discussed are also recorded without explanatory comment. This, while explaining why the special significance of the episode has hitherto passed unnoticed does not, however, cast any very serious doubts upon the existence of the labour shortage which is here treated as being a clue to the justices' policy. For the presentments relating to overpayment are more numerous than any recorded in the North Riding or elsewhere for such a short period.[1] And it also happens that the employers concerned in these presentments are drawn, in the main, from two small areas represented in our burial register sample by parishes with abnormally high mortality for the three years 1679-81.

What conclusions regarding the working of wage assessment machinery under abnormal conditions can be drawn from this episode? It is clear that emphasis must, in the first place, be laid on the delays inherent in the whole procedure of assessment and enforcement. It had originally been laid down, as we have seen, that wages were to be rated at Easter Sessions, or at a sessions held within six weeks after Easter. Where this rule was still adhered to, and where statute sessions were held only once a year, it might, therefore, in the absence of additional sessions, be anything from nine months to a year and a half after an emergency had arisen before a new wage policy could be put into operation and the first batch of those defying that policy proceeded against. Some of the delays might have

[1]Only thirty other cases of overpayment are, as already noticed, recorded in the North Riding minutes for the whole period 1605-1716.

been reduced had it been the practice to require petty constables to bring their bills of masters and servants before the justices, either at Quarter Sessions or "assemblies", instead of having to wait until Martinmas for this necessary information. No hint is, however, contained in the minutes that, on this occasion, any such attempt to short-circuit normal procedure was made. Had statute sessions been held twice a year, too, greater speed in execution might have been achieved. A second conclusion suggested by the evidence is that delays incidental to the observing of customary seasons for assessment and hiring were, as one would expect, amplified by the failure of the officers concerned to carry out their instructions. The chief constables had to be reminded, after the original orders had been issued, to take steps to bring negligent petty constables into line; they themselves, to judge by the wording of the order at Easter Sessions 1680, had been lax in the holding of their statute sessions. The presentments which finally emerged were, as we have seen, highly localized in character, presumably partly because the tendency towards overpayment was stronger in some areas, but probably partly also because of wide variations in the attention paid by different officers to the instructions they received. If adequate records of wage bargains were kept at statute sessions, of course, a partial check on the correctness and completeness of petty constables' bills was provided. This would depend for its value, however, upon the extent to which private unrecorded bargains were entered into. As we have seen, there seems to have been fairly general evasion of the master's duty to attend statute sessions in Holland about this time; so that hiring outside the statutes may have been quite common in North Yorkshire. There are obvious *a priori* reasons for supposing that, in the peculiar conditions of the years under review, private bargains would be increasingly resorted to; and the repeated insistence of the justices on the return of bills by the petty constables is, therefore, understandable. Delays of some of these types were, in the third place, made more serious in their effects by the fact that the justices had, in setting their assessment, to make certain assumptions both regarding future supplies and regarding present supplies; the more serious the delays in determining the extent of non-observance, the slower the discovery of errors in these assumptions, and hence in the assessed rates, was bound to be. The volume of North Riding presentments, coupled with the sanctioning of apparently larger increases in the East Riding rature of 1679, suggests that the North Riding justices had underestimated the extent of the labour shortage; but by the time this was made clear, the emergency itself had almost passed. Altogether, therefore, this Yorkshire episode would seem to show that the machinery of wage assessment was not well adapted to meet short-period fluctuations in labour supply. That the justices should have made the attempt is not, however, surprising, since assessment was, after all, an accepted method of combating "excessive exactions".

In conclusion, it must be emphasized that to admit that the "excessive exactions" aspect of wage assessment was in line with the ideas of the town bourgeoisie and of employers of agricultural labour, and that the justices, as members of these classes, applied assessment in this spirit, is *not* necessarily to admit the justice of the strictures of Thorold Rogers and Cox. For, on the one side, the seventeenth-century wage-earner was not (outside industries such as clothmaking where, in some cases, what American scholars call the dependent phase of the wholesale handicraft stage had been reached) normally solely dependent on wages for his livelihood but could, within limits, offer or withdraw his labour as market conditions warranted. While on the other side, the seventeenth-century employer was not, with the same qualifications, normally a capitalist operating on a large scale, but was often not far removed, in social status and yearly income, from the man he employed. In these circumstances the employer, with wage assessment and other sections of the Statute as his main weapons, was not altogether unequally matched with the worker, whose ability, in fact if not in law, to withdraw his labour or not offer his services or strike a private bargain, provided a formidable defence. In Tawney's words, "the object . . . of assessing wages was not to benefit a privileged oligarchy of employers at the expense of the vast majority of workers, but to protect one class of workers against another".[1]

CHAPTER VII

THE DECAY OF THE SYSTEM

IT would be possible to produce evidence of a sort to
prove either the cessation of wage assessment in the last
quarter of the seventeenth century, or its continuation into
the second half of the eighteenth. On the one hand, the
general impression which an examination of sessions books
leaves on one is very definitely that wage assessment was
not a "live issue" in the eighteenth century; for if it was
in effective operation, how is the absence of proceedings
against those infringing the ratures to be explained? Thus
Hewins long ago advanced the view that the period during
which the Act was effective even to a limited extent practically terminated with the fall of the Stuart monarchy;[1]
while, more recently, Heaton gave it as his opinion that,
for three quarters of a century before its removal from the
Statute book, it had been a shadow without substance.[2]
On the other hand, in some counties the practice of assessing wages showed remarkable tenacity of life. In the East
Riding a new assessment was drawn up in 1722,[3] and there
was a reissue as late as 1757.[4] In Warwickshire reissues continued until 1773,[5] the last reassessment of rates having
been in 1738.[6] In Devonshire there were actually new
scales of wages drawn up in 1732, 1750 and 1778,[7] while

[1]*E.J.* VIII, 345.
[2]*E.J.* XXIV, 232.
[3]East Riding Sessions Books, June 1722.
[4]*Ibid*, April 1757.
[5] Ashby, 176.
[6]*Ibid.*, 175.
[7]Gilboy, 88.

reissues of rates for spinners apparently continued until
1790.[1] In Shropshire the reassessment of 1732 (which
Cunningham, as we have seen, thought was a revival of
the practice to meet special circumstances)[2] was reissued
in the three following years;[3] in 1738 the wording is
doubtful ("order under 5th of Elizabeth"),[4] followed by a
reissue[5] and then no further mention. In Suffolk, after
silence on the matter in the records since 1667, a new
assessment was, as we have seen, apparently issued in
1724[6]; furthermore, proceedings against those infringing
these rates were either taken or contemplated,[7] while the
rates themselves were not merely reissued until 1764,[8] but
the reprinting and distributing of the scale—which would
surely not have been indulged in had reissue been a mere
formality—was undertaken at least up to 1748.[9] Middlesex
reissues continued until 1725, though Dowdell thinks these
were largely a formality,[10] as were, in Heaton's view, the
West Riding reissues up to 1812.[11] There were reassessments
of Gloucestershire wages in 1728[12] and 1732,[13] while the
episode of 1756-7 could almost equally well be advanced as
proof of the vitality of the system,[14] or of its decay. Kent
wages were rated afresh in 1724 and possibly also in 1732,
and one or other of these scales would appear to have been
officially in force as late as 1740.[15] There are also reassessments, dating from the seventeen-twenties or later, for
Nottinghamshire, Lancashire, Westmoreland, Holland,[16]

[1]Hoskins, 130.
[2]*E.J.* IV, 514.
[3]*Salop C.R.* II, 82, 85, 87.
[4]*Ibid.* II, 95.
[5]*Ibid.* II, 98.
[6]Suffolk Order Books, Easter 1727 (Beccles).
[7]Book of Precedents and Indictments, 89.
[8]Suffolk Order Books, April 1764.
[9]*Ibid.* April 1748 (Ipswich).
[10]Dowdell, 150.
[11]*E.J.* XXIV, 232.
[12]Lipson III, 266.
[13]Rogers, *History* VII, 623.
[14]*E.H.R.* XLIII, 402.
[15]*E.H.R.* XLIII, 400-1.
[16]A reissue as late as 1746 is recorded in Holland Q.S. Minutes.

and Buckinghamshire.[1] Faced with known activity of this character, Tawney was led to remark that the view formerly held—that the wage assessment clauses of the Act had become a dead letter by the eighteenth century—was at least not proven.[2]

What are we to make of this somewhat contradictory evidence, of the silence of sessions records in one part of the country accompanied by rating and reissue in another? It is at least clear that there was little uniformity of practice. Even in those districts just reviewed, however, I rather think the vitality of the system in the eighteenth century is disproved by a number of considerations. The first of these is the absence (except in Suffolk) of recorded proceedings against those infringing the assessed rates. By itself this would not, of course, be conclusive, but it is accompanied in the second place by a marked tendency (which was examined at an earlier stage in this study)[3] for eighteenth century assessed and actual rates of wages to diverge from one another. In Middlesex, for instance, though the Court in 1694 took notice of widespread disregard of the assessed rates, not a single case of indictment for overpayment or accepting wages higher than those rates was found in the century 1660-1760.[4] In the third place, there is sometimes evidence that essential complementary parts of the wage assessment policy had fallen into disuse. It is hard to believe, for instance, that attendance at statute sessions was still being enforced in Shropshire when the justices in 1732 stressed the daily inconveniences in connection with settlement and other disputes arising from private contracts, and merely recommended that the terms of the agreement be reduced into writing in the presence of witnesses;[5] otherwise they would surely simply have stated the law—that hirings outside statute sessions were, save in exceptional circumstances, void. Or that they were fulfilling their

[1]See Appendix I.
[2]*V.S.W.* XI, 337.
[3]*Ante,* 22–8.
[4]Dowdell, 150.
[5]*E.J.* IV, 517.

functions adequately in Thetford, where "none hired" was
recorded at the statute sessions held in 1760, 1761, 1763,
1765, and 1766;[1] or in Grimsby, where the number of
hirings at statute sessions had notably diminished by the
end of the seventeenth and the beginning of the eighteenth
centuries.[2] Attendance of petty constables with their
"bills" seems to have varied very much even within the
same county—in the East Riding the Millington constables
regularly recorded in their accounts[3] their charges for
attending the chief constable with the servants' bill in the
seventeen-forties and fifties, but no mention of such activity
is to be found in the Weeton constables' accounts[4] of the
thirties and forties. We have definite knowledge, moreover,
that difficulties were being experienced in keeping statute
sessions alive in the East Riding in the seventeen-thirties.
"A motion being made by Mr. Recorder of York that notice
should be ordered to be given to all the inhabitants of this
Riding that they conform themselves to the Laws in being
in their hiring of servants for the year ensuing, Ordered that
the Clerk of this Court at the next Session recommend to
the Bench to consider of proper means to hinder the Petty
Sessions held by the Chief Constables according to Law
from being disused";[5] there is no evidence, however, of any
further action having been taken in the matter. Clearly,
unless the machinery of statute sessions was in effective
operation, the assessment at least of yearly wages could
hardly be working altogether satisfactorily since the two, as
we have seen, were necessary complements to one another.
Insistence on testimonials seems too, to have been less
emphasized in the later period in many parts of the country;
though this is less significant than the decay of petty sessions.
Finally, contemporary opinion can be advanced to support
the view that wage assessment had fallen into disuse—both
Dowdell and Lipson point out, for instance, that Fielding

[1]Thetford Court Records.
[2]Great Grimsby Court Records.
[3]Millington Constables' Accounts.
[4]Welwick Byelawmen's and Miscellaneous Accounts Book.
[5]East Riding Order Book, November 1731.

(who, as a Middlesex magistrate, is a valuable witness) commented on the utter neglect of the rating of wages in the middle of the eighteenth century.[1]

Turning to the reasons for this development, it cannot, I think, be attributed to the removal of the strong hand of the Council. No doubt, as we have seen, the establishment of minimum rates for clothworkers, and the emphasis on the cost-of-living factor in assessment generally, depended to a large extent on central supervision; but there is no reason to suppose that the rating of wages as a means of preventing excessive exactions conflicted in any way with the views of justices. Why, then, should it have been neglected? Three lines of argument would seem to be possible. Of these the easiest to establish is the first, to the effect that legal obstacles were put in the way of assessment. Holdsworth points out how, by legal decisions of the sixteen-eighties and nineties, a restrictive construction was put upon the Statutes, which were now held to apply only to workers hired by the year;[2] while a better-known decision some years later limited wage assessment to husbandry,[3] and the passing of legislation applying assessment to particular trades[4] must have seemed to confirm this. It is true that, in spite of this, some of the ratures of the later period cover daily wages outside husbandry,[5] but it seems highly improbable that these sections were, or could have been, enforced. Support is, moreover, lent to the view that legal obstacles were deterring the justices from making and enforcing assessments, by some new, but unfortunately incomplete, manuscript evidence. The East Riding justices, as we have seen, revived the practice of assessment in 1722.[6] Two years later[7] the Court requested their Chairman to apply in their names to the Custos Rotulorum, asking him

[1]Dowdell, 151; Lipson III, 264.
[2]Holdsworth, XI, 467.
[3]Lipson III, 263–4.
[4]Holdsworth XI, 467.
[5]*E.g.*, those discussed by Mrs. Gilboy.
[6]East Riding Order Books, April and June 1722.
[7]*Ibid*, October 1724.

if possible to procure an Act of Parliament to enable them the better to execute the powers given them under 5 Elizabeth c. 4, "and that he would also transmit to the Custos Rotulorum a Copy of the Heads of Difficulties in that case touched upon and agreed on at the Sessions held after Michaelmas 1723". Clearly the justices were experiencing difficulties; there is, however, no further mention of them, and a search for a copy of the "heads of difficulties" proved fruitless.

In the second place, it may be suggested that the labour situation with which the justices had to deal was undergoing profound modification. Enclosure, and the contraction of the range of by-employments formerly available, were making it more and more difficult to live at one's own hands. Gradually deprived of this possibility as the eighteenth century advanced, wage-earners both agricultural and otherwise found themselves in a weaker bargaining position, and the danger of excessive exactions was materially lessened; though when they tried to raise their wages by combination, the existence of assessed rates which they had conspired to infringe could always be assumed in taking proceedings against them. If this line of argument is adopted, the paradoxical position is reached that, just when wage assessment could, in theory, have been effectively applied to an increasingly large proportion of the occupied population (because of their increasing dependence on wages) it was discarded as unnecessary. Yet, looked at in one way, this situation is not as paradoxical as it appears at first sight. For if the assessment of wages and the complementary parts of the policy were employed to neutralize the advantages which workers who had opportunities of squatting on the waste or living at their own hands in a variety of ways possessed, then their loss of these advantages would naturally render these special provisions obsolete. Or, putting it in a slightly different way, workers who no longer had the same opportunities of what the authorities were pleased to call "living idly" were led to adopt other forms of resistance, to meet which those in authority had to adopt other means than those provided in the Statute of Artificers. It was not merely that the small class of landless persons was greatly augmented by eighteenth-century developments for, in my view, wage assessment had been devised with that class, amongst others, in mind; but rather that those without land were both larger in numbers and lacked, in large part, even the limited opportunities open to their predecessors. And this, it seems to me, is exactly what happened. Nor does the fact that the legislature applied assessment to certain specified trades in the eighteenth century conflict with this view—there might still, either from a national or a local standpoint, be need for special measures in particular occupations, even when the *general* need for such measures was no longer felt.

For economic historians concerned with general rather than special problems, however, it is necessary to bring the decay of wage assessment into line with general economic and social trends. Viewed from this standpoint, it is not difficult to suggest that, as the rise of a class of business leaders and the adequate performance of the entrepreneur function meant the sweeping away of hindrances to freedom of contract, the rating of wages had to go. The language used by the clothiers in the course of the 1756 Gloucestershire dispute was, as Lipson has pointed out,[1] significant. And though it is worth remembering that this language was employed when the use of assessment to deprive clothiers of their freedom to scale wages *downwards* was involved, it is clear that the fixing of maxima, too, was a curb on the activities of entrepreneurs who must, if they were to make full use of their talents, be free to offer higher rates than their competitors, for labour as for anything else, when the occasion arose. It seems to me, however, that a generalized argument on these lines is highly dangerous. The question at issue, after all, was the rating of wages in a small range of occupations which, except for the clothing group, did not include trades in which, in the eighteenth

[1] Lipson III, 268–9.

century, capitalistic forms had yet developed far enough to make the employers involved feel that their activities were unduly circumscribed by the imposition of maximum wages which could be adjusted from year to year as required. If the legislature, as Lipson has warned us,[1] was not sufficiently conscious of the need for freedom in economic relationships to refrain from applying wage assessment to a variety of trades by different eighteenth-century statutes, it is hardly to be supposed that the justices up and down the country abandoned this procedure as being out of conformity with the necessities of an expanding economy. Had they felt the need for wage assessment and its corollaries, they would not have been deterred from reviving it by anything less concrete than legal decisions limiting the scope of their activities. Presumably, therefore, they were either impeded by these legal obstacles or, as suggested above, wages could now be kept at the required level without the aid of the machinery of assessment.

There remains, it is true, the awkward problem as to what lay behind these legal decisions. One eminent authority has recently said that the courts "having regard to the prevailing economic conditions and the current of economic opinion, construed the Statutes [relating to wage assessment] restrictively".[2] To subscribe to this proposition would seem, however, to involve giving an affirmative answer to at least three questions. Did prevailing economic conditions at the time of the decisions demand as restrictive an interpretation as the courts gave? Was the current of economic opinion at that time so definitely set towards complete freedom in economic relationships? Were the courts more likely to be influenced by such factors than the local magistrates or the central legislature? Each of these questions would have to be examined separately in the light of the available evidence, it seems to me, before the proposition could be regarded as finally established. Moreover, any explanation of the cases under consideration which did

[1] Lipson III, 270.
[2] Holdsworth XI, 467.

not, with suitable adaptation, explain also the 1598 decision (whereby, despite 5 Elizabeth c. 4, a remedy was provided for workers in husbandry whose masters detained their wages) *and* the nineteenth and early twentieth-century animus of the courts against trade unions, would be unsatisfactory. It might be possible to show that all these decisions were in line with the economic interests of those charged with the administration and interpretation of the law in the different periods involved. Here, as in so many other instances, the need for co-operation between research workers in legal and economic history is self-evident.

APPENDIX I

A LIST of wage assessments under 5 Elizabeth c. 4, and
amending statutes, omitting London (for which see
E.H.R. XV, 445-55, *E.J.* X, 404-11, and Tawney and
Power I, 363-70) and Sussex (for which Miss Hindmarsh's
thesis should be consulted). Reissues without alteration
have, as far as possible, been excluded, though some probably still remain. Assessments marked with an asterisk
were not mentioned in Lipson III, 256-7, 260, 262-3; while
those included in Lipson's list, which are here excluded for
some reason, are given in italics. Those enclosed in square
brackets are mentioned in Miss Hindmarsh's thesis, and are
based on evidence which I have not myself seen; as the
definition of a reissue which she uses differs from mine, an
unknown proportion of these may, in fact, be what are here
treated as reissues. An attempt is made to indicate whether
the most accessible printed version is a reasonably complete
and accurate copy of the *rates* given in the source ("full"),
or whether only a selection is provided ("partial"). Where
no printed version apparently exists, an owner or custodian
is mentioned, if the actual assessment is known to have
been in existence within the last fifty years or so. Some
assessments are included of which no copy now survives
("evidence only"), but only where there is reason to
believe that reassessment, and not merely reissue, was
involved.

*[1563 COVENTRY Rates given in Hindmarsh, 164]
 1563 EXETER In custody of Town Clerk, Exeter
              (preamble only)
* 1563 HOLLAND Copy of Proclamation at Queen's
               College, Oxford

1563   KENT   *E.H.R.* XLI, 270-3 (full)

1563   LINCOLN   (City) *V.C.H.Lincs.* II, 330 (full)

* 1563   MAIDSTONE   *Archaeologia Cantiana* XXII, 316-9 (full)

1563   RUTLAND   Rogers, *History* IV, 120-3 (full). The assessment that Cunningham, 894, dates 1564 is apparently this one wrongly dated—he gives a Bodleian reference, and this is the only Rutland assessment of the period in their possession.

1563   SOUTHAMPTON (Town and County)   Copy of Proclamation (preamble only) in Bodleian Library—Arch.G.c.6 (88b). Cunningham, 894, gives 1564 as date and a Bodleian reference. They only have this one, however.

1564   EXETER   *H.M.C.Exeter*, 50-1 (full)

* 1570   CHESTER   Morris, 367-8 (partial)

1570   HULL   Copy of Proclamation in the British Museum copy of Dyson

1576   CANTERBURY   Copy of Proclamation in Municipal Library, Canterbury

*[1578   CAMBRIDGESHIRE   Mentioned Hindmarsh, p. xxvii]

*[1580   HERTFORDSHIRE   Mentioned Hindmarsh, 57.   Minor changes apparently took place in 1581, 1592 and 1594]

1592   HERTFORDSHIRE   *Hertford County Records* I, 8-12 (full)

1593   CHESTER   Both Rogers, *History* VI, 685-6 (incorrectly headed 1591) and Eden III, p. xciii, print this assessment, but in each case there are serious errors and omissions. Morris, 367-8 (full), is more reliable.

1593   E.R.YORKS   Rogers, *History* VI, 686-9 (full): one or two minor discrepancies between this and *Tudor and Stuart Proclamations* I, 96 (partial)

1594   CANTERBURY   *Tudor and Stuart Proclamations* I, 97 (partial).   Copy of Proclamation in Municipal Library, Canterbury.

1594 DEVONSHIRE Hamilton, 12-13 (full)

1594 ESSEX Webb, 455, evidence only. Almost certainly a reissue

1595 CARDIGANSHIRE *Tudor and Stuart Proclamations* I, 98 (full)

1595 HIGHAM FERRERS Copy of Proclamation in Society of Antiquaries Library, London—2 (102)

1595 LANCASTER (County) *Tudor and Stuart Proclamations* I, 98 (partial). Rogers, *History* VI, 689-91 (full)

1595 NEW SARUM *Tudor and Stuart Proclamations* I, 98 (partial). Copy of Proclamation at Queen's College, Oxford (331 B)

1596 CHESTER Eden III, pp. xciv-v (full). Rogers, *History* VI, 685-6 (incorrectly headed 1594, and with errors and omissions). Morris, 367-8 (full)

* 1597 CHESTER Morris, 367-8 (full)

*[1598 ESSEX Mentioned Hindmarsh, 49]

1602 WILTSHIRE *H.M.C.Various* I, 162 (full). Proposed by weavers and clothiers, confirmed by Justices.

1603 WILTSHIRE *H.M.C.Various* I, 162-7 (full): also Bland, 345-50, wrongly headed 1604.

1605 NORFOLK *E.H.R.* XIII, 523-7 (full)

*[1607 STAFFORDSHIRE Rates given in Hindmarsh, 61-3]

1610 RUTLAND (?Oakham) Rogers, *History* VI, 691-3 (full)
The twelfth assessment in Knoop and Jones, *Medieval Mason*, 239 is a misprint: nothing is known of a Surrey assessment of this date.

*[1611 ESSEX Mentioned Hindmarsh, 49]

* 1612 ESSEX Listed in *H.M.C. County of Essex*, 491. Rates given in Hindmarsh, 61-3.

1619 KESTEVEN In possession of Duke of Rutland at Belvoir Castle, 1888, according to *H.M.C. Rutland* I, 455. Rates given in Hindmarsh, 64.

*[1620 and 1621 STAFFORDSHIRE Mentioned Hindmarsh, 47, 50]

* 1621 FAVERSHAM *Archaeologia Cantiana* XVI, 270 (full)

1621 KESTEVEN *H.M.C. Rutland* I, 460-2 (full)

1630 SUFFOLK (Bury Division only?) *E.H.R.* XII, 307-11 (full)

1630 NORWICH Evidence only. (Improbable, see text)

1631 HERTFORDSHIRE (Liberty of St. Albans). Clutterbuck I, pp. xxii-xxiv (full). Lipson III, 257, following *V.C.H.Herts.* IV, 228 and *St. Albans Corporation Records*, 280-2 (where an unreliable summary is given) wrongly dates this assessment 1632.

1631 HERTFORDSHIRE (One Division?). In custody of Town Clerk, Hertford. Previously given as for Hertford, I feel certain on inspection that it is really for Hertfordshire, probably for one division only.

1632 GLOUCESTER Rogers, *History* VI, 694 (full)

1632 HEREFORDSHIRE *H.M.C. Portland* III, 31 (full)

1633 DORSET Roberts, 207-10 (full)

1634 DERBYSHIRE *V.C.H. Derbyshire* II, 183 (partial). Cox II, 239-40 (full)

*[1634 DORSET Rates given in Hindmarsh, 66-8]

* 1634 NORWICH Norwich Sessions Records. Evidence only

1635 WILTSHIRE *H.M.C.Various* I, 169 (full)

*[1636 NOTTINGHAMSHIRE Mentioned Hindmarsh, 47]

* 1640 NORWICH Norwich Sessions Records. Evidence only

* 1641 STAFFORDSHIRE Staffordshire Sessions Books, Easter 1641. Evidence only

* 1642 PORTSMOUTH *Portsmouth Records*, 161-2

* 1647 SOMERSET *Somerset Q.S. Records* III, 40 (full)

1647 W.R.YORKS *E.J.* XXIV, 221-4 (full)

1648 DERBYSHIRE *V.C.H. Derbyshire* II, 183 (partial). Cox II, 240-2 (full)

1648 NOTTINGHAMSHIRE *Journal of George Fox* (1902 reprint) I, 27. Evidence only

* 1648 SOMERSET *Somerset Q.S. Records* III, 66-7 (full)

* 1648 or 1649 STAFFORDSHIRE Staffordshire Sessions Books, Easter 1648 (or 9). Evidence only

* 1650 NORWICH Norwich Sessions Records. Evidence only

1651 ESSEX Rogers, *History* VI, 694-7 (full): Eden III, pp. xcviii-ci (full): *Essex Review* XLIII, 10-11 (partial). Minor discrepancies in rates between these three.

* 1651 SOMERSET *Somerset Q.S. Records* III, 150-1 (full)

* 1652 SOMERSET *Somerset Q.S. Records* III, 176-7 (full)

* 1653 SOMERSET *Somerset Q.S. Records* III, 211 (full)

1654 DEVON Hamilton, 163-4 (full)

* 1654 SOMERSET *Somerset Q.S. Records* III, 236 (full)

* 1655 GLOUCESTER Rogers, *History* VI, 694 (full)

* 1655 SOMERSET *Somerset Q.S. Records* III, 263 (full)

1655 WILTSHIRE *H.M.C.Various* I, 169-73 (full). Some of the rates given differ from *Wilts C.R.*, 290-4 (full)

* 1656 STAFFORDSHIRE Staffordshire Sessions Books, Easter 1656 (full)

*[1656 SUFFOLK Mentioned Hindmarsh, 223]

* 1657 NORWICH Printed in text, 9

* 1657 WARWICKSHIRE Ashby, 170-1 (full)

1658 N.R.YORKS *N.R.Q.S.R.* VI, 3-5 (full)

1661 ESSEX Rogers, *History* VI, 697-8 (full)

* 1661 NORFOLK Norfolk Q.S. Minutes say some wages were increased

* 1662 NORFOLK Norfolk Q.S. Minutes say wages were "published and made"

1662 WORCESTERSHIRE *H.M.C.Various* I, 323 (full)

* 1666 SOMERSET *Somerset Q.S. Records* IV, 13 (full)
  1667 NORTHAMPTONSHIRE *Econ.H.R.* I, 133-4 (full)
* 1668 SOMERSET *Somerset Q.S. Records* IV, 43 (full)
* 1669 E.R.YORKS *E.H.R.* LII, 283-9 (full)
* 1669 HULL In custody of Town Clerk, Hull
*[1669 KENT Mentioned Hindmarsh, p. xxviii. Others for 1686 and 1687]
* 1669 LINDSEY (All Divisions) Lindsey Q.S. Minutes. Definite evidence—"new rates of wages agreed upon and confirmed at this sessions for the whole parts of Lindsey"—but no assessment has survived.
* 1669 SOMERSET *Somerset Q.S. Records* IV, 61 (full)
  166- MIDDLESEX Cunningham III, 887-93 (full)
* 1671 SOMERSET *Somerset Q.S. Records* IV, 99 (full)
  1671 or 1672 W.R.YORKS *E.J.* XXIV, 229 (partial)
*[1672 DURHAM (County) Mentioned in Hindmarsh. Others for 1674, 6, 7, 8 and 9]
* 1672 SOMERSET *Somerset Q.S. Records* IV, 116 (full)
* 1672 WARWICKSHIRE Ashby, 172-3 (full)
* 1673 BUCKINGHAMSHIRE *Bucks. Sessions Records* I, 149-50. Doubtful evidence
*[1673 NORTHAMPTONSHIRE Mentioned Hindmarsh, p. xxviii. Another for 1675]
* 1673 SOMERSET *Somerset Q.S. Records* IV, 134 (full)
* 1676 BUCKINGHAMSHIRE *Bucks. Sessions Records* I, 29, 52, 71, 121. Evidence only
* 1676 HOLLAND (work on sewers). Copy in Parish Chest at Sutterton
* 1676 SOMERSET *Somerset Q.S. Records* IV, 202 (full)
* 1677 BURY ST. EDMUNDS *East Anglian Miscellany* I, 87 (full)
* 1677 SOMERSET *Somerset Q.S. Records* IV, 224 (full)
  1678 HERTFORDSHIRE *Hertford C.R.* I, 292 (full)
* 1679 DEVONSHIRE Mentioned Hoskins, 130
* 1679 E.R.YORKS (Ouse and Derwent Division only?) *E.H.R.* LII, 283-9 (full)

1680 HOLLAND (Certain Hundreds only)   *V.C.H.*
        Lincolnshire II, 336 (partial): Thompson, 761-6
        (full)

1680 N.R.YORKS   *N.R.Q.S.R.*   VII, 45   (partial).
        Original missing.

1682 BURY ST. EDMUNDS (or SUFFOLK, Bury
        Division?) Rogers, *History* VI, 698-9 (full)

* 1683 HULL (may be for 1678, however). In custody of
        Town Clerk, Hull

   1684 WARWICKSHIRE Rogers, History VI, 699-700 (full).
        Almost certainly a reissue. Rates are the same as 1672
        assessment except for those for the chief hind and
        shepherd which, as given by Rogers, seem highly
        improbable.

*[1684 NORTHAMPTONSHIRE   Mentioned Hind-
        marsh, p. xxviii]

* 1684 W.R.YORKS   *E.J.* XXIV, 229 (partial)

   1685 SOMERSET   *H.M.C.* VII, 698-9 (full)

*[1685 and 1686 STAFFORDSHIRE Mentioned in Hind-
        marsh]

   1685 WILTSHIRE   *H.M.C.Various* I, 174-5 (full). One
        of the rates given differs from *Wilts. C.R.*, 294-6
        (full)

   1687 BUCKINGHAMSHIRE *Bucks. Sessions Records* I,
        227-9 (full).   The summary given in *V.C.H.*
        Bucks. II, 71, differs in some rates.

* 1687 HERTFORDSHIRE *Hertford C.R.* VI, 400-4 (full)

* 1687 OXFORDSHIRE   Gretton, pp. lxiii-lxiv (full).
        Mention is made in Hindmarsh of assessments
        for eight of the last nine years of the century.

* 1688 BUCKINGHAMSHIRE *Bucks. Sessions Records* I,
        262 (full)

*[1689 STAFFORDSHIRE Mentioned in Hindmarsh]

* 1690 BUCKINGHAMSHIRE *Bucks. Sessions Records* I,
        337 (full). Mention is made in Hindmarsh of
        assessments for all remaining years of the century.

* 1690 KESTEVEN   *Kesteven Q.S. Minutes*, 364.   Evi-
        dence only

9

* 1693   HERTFORDSHIRE   *Hertford C.R.* VI, 460 (full)

*[1695   KENT   Mentioned in Hindmarsh]

* 1695   W.R.YORKS   *E.J.* XXIV, 229 (partial)

*[1697   BUCKINGHAMSHIRE   Mentioned in Hind-
        marsh]

*[1699   WORCESTER   Mentioned in Hindmarsh]

* 1701   DEVONSHIRE   Gilboy, 88-9, 110-11 (partial)

* 1701   OXFORDSHIRE   Gilboy, 89, 110 (partial)

  1703   *W.R.YORKS   Rogers, History VII, 610-2 (full):
        merely a reissue, see E.J. XXIV, 229*

  1706   *W.R.YORKS   Rogers, History VII, 614: merely a
        reissue, see E.J. XXIV, 232*

* 1708   HERTFORDSHIRE   *Hertford C.R.* VII, 85 (full)

  1710   WARWICKSHIRE   *V.C.H. Warwickshire* II, 180
        (full).   Only two rates differ from 1672 assess-
        ment.

  1713   *DEVONSHIRE   Hamilton 273 (full).   Probably a
        reissue: see Gilboy, 88.   Wrongly given as 1712 in
        Cunningham, 896*

* 1714   HOLLAND   Holland Q.S. Minutes, Easter 1714
        (full)

* 1719   KENDAL   *Ars Quatuor Coronatorum* X, 32-3 (full),
        also *Econ.H.R.* III, 358 (partial)

* 1721   HULL   In custody of Town Clerk, Hull

* 1722   E.R.YORKS   Definite evidence in E.R.Order
        Book

  1722   *W.R.YORKS   Rogers, History VII, 614, merely a re-
        issue, see E.J. XXIV, 232*

* 1723   NOTTINGHAMSHIRE   Chambers, 281-3 (par-
        tial)

  1724   KENT   *E.H.R.* XLIII, 270-3 (full)

  1724   NOTTINGHAMSHIRE   *V.C.H. Notts.* II, 295
        (partial).   Apparently not a reissue of the assess-
        ment discussed by Chambers, as some of the
        rates given differ.

* 1724   NOTTINGHAMSHIRE   Copnall, 65 (full).   A
        different assessment from that given in *V.C.H.
        Notts.* II, 295. (Possibly for a different division?)

* 1724 SUFFOLK Evidence (Suffolk Q.S. Order Book, April 1727)

  1725 LANCASHIRE (County) *Annals of Agriculture* XXV, 305-15 (full)

*[1727 DORSET Mention is made in Hindmarsh, p. xxvii, of assessments for 1729, 38 and 57 also]

  1728 GLOUCESTERSHIRE Lipson III, 266, discusses but does not give rates. Hewins, 160, prints weavers' assessed rates for 1727: should this be 1728?

*[1730 OXFORDSHIRE Mentioned in Hindmarsh, but not in Gilboy]

* 1730 WARWICKSHIRE Ashby, 174 (full)

* 1731 HOLLAND Holland Q.S. Minutes, May 1731. Evidence only

* 1732 DEVONSHIRE Gilboy 88-9, 110-11 (partial) (possibly a reissue)

  1732 GLOUCESTER Rogers, *History* VII, 623 (full)

  1732 KENT Rogers, *History* VII, 623 (full). Rates doubtful—see *E.H.R.* XLIII, 400-1

  1732 SHROPSHIRE *E.J.* IV, 516-8 (full). Differs slightly from assessment printed *Salop C.R.* II, 79, probably due to errors in the latter

* 1738 WARWICKSHIRE Ashby, 175 (full): Bland, 546-7 (full)

* 1750 DEVONSHIRE Gilboy, 88-9, 110-11 (partial)

  1750 WESTMORELAND In possession of S. H. Le Fleming Esq. at Rydal Hall about 1890, according to *H.M.C. Le Fleming*, 367

  1754 HOLLAND Thompson, 766-7 (partial)

  1756 GLOUCESTERSHIRE *House of Commons Journals* XXVII, 732 (full)

  1765 BUCKINGHAMSHIRE *V.C.H. Bucks.* II, 84 (partial)

  1765 WARWICKSHIRE *V.C.H. Warwickshire II, 181 (full). Merely a reissue of the 1738 assessment.*

* 1778 DEVONSHIRE Gilboy, 88-9, 110-11 (partial)

APPENDIX II

Summary of the relevant sections of 5 Elizabeth c. 4.
(The reader who has access to Tawney and Power, or to
Bland, will naturally refer to the document itself rather than
to this inadequate summary).

I   Previous laws limiting wages have been rendered
out-of-date by the advancement of prices. If the
principles of such of these laws as are meet to be
continued are brought together in one law, this
should "banish idleness, advance husbandry, and
yield unto the hired person both in the time of
scarcity and in the time of plenty a convenient
proportion of wages". All previous statutes on the
hiring, departing, working, and wages of servants
are therefore repealed.

II   No-one to be retained for less than one whole year
in any of certain enumerated occupations.

III   Every person unmarried, and everyone under
thirty, who has been brought up, or has engaged
for three years or more, in one of these occupations,
and who does not fulfil a minimum property
qualification and is not already retained shall,
upon request, serve anyone requiring them to do
so in that occupation.

IV   No person to put away a servant and no servant to
depart before the end of his term unless it be for
some reasonable cause to be allowed before a
justice, to whom any of the parties grieved shall
complain. No putting away or departing at the
end of term without one quarter warning given.

V   Everyone between twelve and sixty not otherwise
        lawfully retained or coming under various exemp-
        tions is compellable to serve in husbandry by the
        year.

VI   Penalty on masters unduly dismissing servants,
        40s.; on servants unduly departing or refusing to
        serve, imprisonment.

VII   No servant to depart out of the parish where he
        was last retained without a testimonial under the
        seal of the constable and two other honest house-
        holders, declaring his lawful departure.   This
        testimonial to be delivered to the servant and
        registered by the parson.

VIII   Penalty on a servant departing without such testi-
        monial, imprisonment or whipping; on anyone
        hiring him, £5.

IX   Hours of work for day labourers laid down.

X   Penalty on artificers etc. breaking contracts with
        employers, imprisonment and fine of £5.

XI   Justices, mayor, etc. to rate wages of any workers
        on a time- or piece-rate basis at every general
        sessions within six weeks after Easter, calling unto
        them such discreet and grave persons as they shall
        think meet, and conferring together respecting the
        plenty or scarcity of the time and other circum-
        stances necessary to be considered.   Provisions
        regarding certifying of such assessments into
        Chancery and the proclaiming of the rates locally,
        as well as for reissue in lieu of reassessment.

XII   Penalty on justices absent from sessions for rating
        wages, £5.

XIII   Penalty for giving wages higher than the rate, ten
        days' imprisonment and fine of £5; for receiving
        the same, twenty-one days' imprisonment.

XV   At harvest time justices or constables may cause all
        such artificers and persons as be meet to labour to
        do daily harvest work.   Penalty for persons
        refusing, imprisonment in the stocks.

XVI   Those going harvesting in other counties must have a "temporary absence" certificate from a justice.

XVII   Mayor or two justices may compel any unmarried woman between twelve and forty not already in service to do any suitable work.

XXX   Justices in their divisions to meet twice yearly to see to the execution of the Statute.

XXXI   Justices at such sessions to be allowed 5s. per day.

BIBLIOGRAPHY

I. Manuscript Sources (arranged under places of deposit)

ALDEBURGH (Suffolk): Town Clerk
  Miscellaneous Aldeburgh Sessions Papers, late 16th and
  early 17th centuries.
BEVERLEY: Clerk of the Peace for the East Riding
  East Riding Sessions Books 1647-51 and 1708 onwards
BEVERLEY: Town Clerk
  Miscellaneous Beverley Sessions Papers, 17th and 18th
  centuries
BOSTON: Clerk of the Peace for Holland
  Holland Q.S. Minutes 1673 onwards
  Sessions Rolls sampled
EVERINGHAM (East Riding): The Dowager Duchess of
  Norfolk. Philip Constable's Account Book 1672-92
GRIMSBY: Town Clerk
  Miscellaneous Sessions Papers covering most of the
  period under review
HEDON (East Riding): Mayor
  Miscellaneous Sessions Papers for some parts of the 17th
  century
HERTFORD: Town Clerk
  Miscellaneous Sessions Papers 1627 onwards
HULL: University College Library
  Welwick (East Riding) Byelaw Men's and Miscellaneous
  Accounts Book 1651-1764
HULL: Town Clerk
  Hull Sessions Books 18th century
  Wage Assessments separately filed

123

IPSWICH : Clerk of the Peace for East Suffolk
Suffolk Q.S. Minute Books 1650-67 and 1674 onwards
Suffolk Q.S. Order Books 1639-51 and 1658 onwards
Book of Precedents and Indictments (a justice's note-book
of the early 18th century)
Sessions Rolls sampled

IPSWICH : Public Library
Extracts transcribed from the Ipswich Sessions Books by
V. B. Redstone
Diary of Devreux Edgar, a Suffolk magistrate, early
18th century

IPSWICH : Town Clerk
Ipswich Sessions Books covering practically the whole of
the period under review

LINCOLN : Clerk of the Peace for Lindsey
Lindsey Q.S. Minutes 1665-78, 1704-12 and 1738
onwards
Sessions Rolls sampled

LINCOLN : J. W. F. Hill, Esq.
Transcript of Lincoln Q.S. Minutes 1657-62 and 1668

LONDON : Public Record Office
Privy Council Register

MASHAM (West Riding) : Parish Chest
Masham Churchwardens' Accounts 1542-1678

MILLINGTON (East Riding) : Parish Chest
Millington Constables' Accounts 1700 onwards

NORWICH : City Muniment Room
Norwich Sessions Books covering practically the whole of
the period under review
Sessions Rolls sampled

NORWICH : Clerk of the Peace for Norfolk
Norfolk Q.S. Books of Proceedings 1639-44, 1649-54,
1661-76 and 1683 onwards
Norfolk Q.S. Order Books 1650 onwards
Sessions Rolls sampled

RUDSTON (East Riding) : Sir Godfrey Macdonald of the
Isles

Captain Bosseville's Account Book (relating to Penistone, West Riding)

SCARBOROUGH: Town Clerk

Miscellaneous Scarborough Sessions Papers 17th and 18th centuries

Miscellaneous Scarborough Corporation Accounts

STAFFORD: Clerk of the Peace for Staffordshire

Staffordshire Sessions Books 1619-30, 1640-67 and 1687 onwards

Sessions Rolls sampled

THETFORD (Norfolk): Town Clerk

Thetford Sessions Books 1570-90, 1610-29, 1632-9 and 1751 onwards

TOPCLIFFE (West Riding): Parish Chest

Topcliffe Churchwardens' Accounts 1652 onwards

WAKEFIELD: Clerk of the Peace for the West Riding

West Riding Sessions Books sampled

II.   Printed Sources and Secondary Authorities

No bibliography of printed materials on this subject could be called "complete" unless it included, *inter alia*, every treatise on the practice of justices of the peace, and every work in which merely incidental reference was made to the subject under review. No attempt is here made to achieve completeness of this kind, this bibliography being merely intended to provide a reference list of those works mentioned in the course of the present study. Some slight modification in the order of words has been made in a few titles, so that footnote references may be more easily found.

(a) *Books*:

Acts of the Privy Council

Annals of Agriculture, ed. A. Young (1784-1808)

Archaeologia Cantiana, XVI, XXII

Ashby, A. W., One Hundred Years of Poor Law Administra-

tion in a Warwickshire Village (Oxford Studies in Social and Legal History, III) (1912)

Bedfordshire County Records, II. (Calendar of the Sessions Minute Books 1651-1660) (N.D.)

Bland, A. E., Brown, P. A., and Tawney, R. H., *English Economic History : Select Documents* (1914)

Book of John Fisher, 1580-88, (Town Clerk and Deputy Recorder of Warwick) ed. T. Kemp. (N.D.)

Buckinghamshire Sessions Records, I. 1678-1694 ed. W. Le Hardy (1933)

Burn, R., *Justice of the Peace* (1756 edition)

Calendars of State Papers Domestic

Chambers, J. D., *Nottinghamshire in the Eighteenth Century* (1932)

Clark, G. N., *The Later Stuarts, 1660-1714* (1934)

Clutterbuck, R., *The History and Antiquities of the County of Hertford*, I, (1815)

Copnall, H. H., *Nottinghamshire County Records* (17th Century) (1915)

Cowell, J., *The Interpreter, or the signification of words* (1658 edition)

Cox, J. C., *Three Centuries of Derbyshire Annals*, I-II, (1890)

Creighton, C., *A History of Epidemics in Britain* (1891)

Cunningham, W., *The Growth of English Industry and Commerce* (1882)

Dalton, M., *Countrey Justice* (1697 edition)

Davies, G., *The Early Stuarts, 1603-1660* (1937)

Dowdell, E. G., *A Hundred Years of Quarter Sessions* (1932)

Dyson, H., *Proclamation Book* (1618) (British Museum, G. 6463)

Eden, F. M., *The State of the Poor* (1797) (The abridgement of 1928 omits wage assessments)

Furley, J. S., *Quarter Sessions Government in Hampshire in the Seventeenth Century* (1937)

Farming Books of Henry Best, 1641 (Surtees Society, XXXIII) (1857)

Gilboy, E. W., *Wages in Eighteenth-Century England* (1934)

Gretton, M. S., *Oxfordshire Justices of the Peace in the*

Seventeenth Century (Oxfordshire Record Society XVI) (1934)

Hamilton, A. H. A., *Quarter Sessions from Queen Elizabeth to Queen Anne* (1878)

Hampson, E. M., *The Treatment of Poverty in Cambridge-shire, 1597-1834* (1934)

Heaton, H., *The Yorkshire Woollen and Worsted Industries* (1920)

Hertford County Records, I, 1581-1698 ed. W. J. Hardy (1905)

Hertford County Records, V-VIII, 1619-1799 ed. W. Le Hardy (1928-35)

Hewins, W. A. S., *English Trade and Finance* (1892)

Hindmarsh, N., The Assessment of Wages by the Justices of the Peace, 1563-1700. London University Ph.D. thesis (typescript) (1932)

Historical Manuscripts Commission: Reports

Holdsworth, W. S., *A History of English Law* IV, VI (1924): X, XI (1938)

Hoskins, W. G., *Industry and Trade in Exeter 1688-1800* (1935)

Justice's Case Law (1731)

Kesteven Quarter Sessions Minutes, 1674-95 ed. S. A. Peyton (Lincoln Record Society, XXV, XXVI) (1931)

Knoop, D. and Jones, G. P., *The London Mason in the Seventeenth Century* (1935)

Knoop, D. and Jones, G. P., *The Medieval Mason* (1933)

Lancashire Quarter Sessions Records, I. Rolls 1590-1606 ed. J. Tait (Chetham Society LXXVII new series) (1917)

Leonard, E. M., *The Early History of English Poor Relief* (1900)

Lipson, E., *Economic History of England*, III (1931) (The relevant sections of his earlier book on the English woollen and worsted industries are reproduced here)

Manchester Sessions, I, 1616-1622-1623 ed. E. Axon (Lancashire and Cheshire Record Society, XLII) (1901)

Marshall, D., *The English Poor in the Eighteenth Century* (1926)

Middlesex County Records, I-IV ed. J. C. Jeaffreson (Middlesex County Records Society 1886-1892)

Middlesex County Records: Calendar of Sessions Books 1689-1709 ed. W. J. Hardy (1905)

Middlesex Sessions Records, New Series, I, 1612-1614 ed. W. Le Hardy (1935)

Morris, R. H., *Chester in the Plantagenet and Tudor Reigns* (N.D.)

North Riding Quarter Sessions Records, 1605-1786 ed. J. C. Atkinson (North Riding Record Society, Old Series I-IX) (1884-1892)

Northamptonshire Quarter Sessions Records, 1630, 1657, 1657-8 ed. J. Wake (Northamptonshire Record Society, I) (1924)

Norwich City Records, II, ed. W. Hudson and J. C. Tingey (1910)

Portsmouth Records Extracts, ed. R. East (1891)

Putnam, B. H., *Early Treatises on the Practice of the Justices of the Peace* (1924)

Roberts, G., *The Social History of the People of the Southern Counties of England in Past Centuries* (1856)

Rogers, J. E. T., *A History of Agriculture and Prices in England* III-VII (1882-1902)

Rogers, J. E. T., *Six Centuries of Work and Wages* (1909 edition)

St. Albans Corporation Records, ed. A. E. Gibbs (1890)

Shropshire County Records. Orders of Shropshire Quarter Sessions, I-II, 1638-1782, ed. R. L. Kenyon.

Somerset Quarter Sessions Records, I-IV, ed. E. H. B. Harbin and M. C. B. Dawes (Somerset Record Society, XXIII, XXIV, XXVIII, XXXIV) (1907-1919)

Staffordshire Quarter Sessions Rolls, I-III, 1581-1597, ed. S. A. H. Burne (Collections for a History of Staffordshire) (1931-1933)

Surrey Record Society XIII-XIV (Quarter Sessions Records 1659-1663) ed. H. Jenkinson and D. L. Powell (1934-5)

Tawney, R. H. and Power, E. E., *Tudor Economic Documents*, I-III (1924)

Thompson, P., *The History and Antiquities of Boston* (1856)

Tudor and Stuart Proclamations 1485-1714, I, ed. R. Steele (1910)

Unwin, G., *Industrial Organisation in the Sixteenth and Seventeenth Centuries* (1904)

Victoria County Histories

Warwick County Records I, 1625-37 ed. S. C. Ratcliff and H. C. Johnson (1935)

Webb, S. and B., *English Local Government: The Parish and the County* (1924)

West Riding Sessions Rolls, 1597-8-1602 ed. J. Lister (Yorks. Arch. Socy., Record Series, III) (1888)

West Riding Sessions Records, 1611-42 ed. J. Lister (Yorks. Arch. Socy., Record Series, LIV) (1915)

Wiltshire County Records of the Seventeenth Century ed. B. H. Cunnington (1932)

Worcestershire County Records. Quarter Sessions Rolls I-II, 1591-1643 ed. J. W. W. Bund (1899-1900)

(*b*) *Articles*

Barber, F., "The West Riding Sessions Rolls" *Yorkshire Archaeological Journal*, V, 362-405

Benham, W. G., "Essex Wages in Cromwell's time" *Essex Review*, XLIII, 10-11

Cunningham, W., "Dr. Cunningham and his Critics" *Economic Journal*, IV, 508-18

Dare, M. P., "Old-Time Lawkeepers, a Study of the Constables of Ayleston, Co. Leics." *Assoc. Arch. Soc. Rep.*, XXXVIII, 148

Heaton, H., "The Assessment of Wages in the West Riding of Yorkshire in the Seventeenth and Eighteenth Centuries" *Economic Journal*, XXIV, 218-35

Hewins, W. A. S., "The Regulation of Wages by the Justices of the Peace" *Economic Journal*, VIII, 340-6

Hutchins, B. L., "The Regulation of Wages by Guilds and Town Authorities" *Economic Journal*, X, 404-11

Kelsall, R. K., "Two East Yorkshire Wage Assessments 1669, 1679" *English Historical Review*, LII, 283-9

Leonard, E. M., "The Relief of the Poor by the State Regulation of Wages" *English Historical Review*, XIII, 91-3

McArthur, E. A., "The Regulation of Wages in the Sixteenth Century" *English Historical Review*, XV, 445-55

Putnam, B. H., "Lambard's 'Eirenarcha' and a Kent Wage Assessment of 1563" *English Historical Review*, XLI, 260-73

Putnam, B. H., "Northamptonshire Wage Assessments of 1560 and 1667" *Economic History Review*, I, 124-34

Roberts, R. A., "The Borough Business of a Suffolk Town (Orford), 1559-1660" *Royal Historical Society Transactions* (4th series), XIV, 95-120

Tawney, R. H., "The Assessment of Wages in England by the Justices of the Peace" *Vierteljahrschrift für Sozial- und Wirtschaftsgeschichte*, XI, 307-37, 533-64

Tingey, J. C., "An Assessment of Wages for the County of Norfolk in 1610" *English Historical Review*, XIII, 522-7

Waterman, E. L., "Some New Evidence on Wage Assessments in the Eighteenth Century" *English Historical Review*, XLIII, 398-408

INDEX

Assemblies, additional, 54–61
Assessments, wage, area covered
    by, 3–6
— — cessation of in 18th
    century, 102–4
— — cost-of-living and assessed
    rates in, 69–78
— — cost-of-living statements
    contained in, 67–9
— — distinguished from re-
    issues, 6–7
— — drawing-up, advice taken
    in, 88–9
— — — joint action in, 11–3
— — — periods of activity in,
    13–4
— — — sessions for, 2–3
— — effectiveness of, 15–28
— — for whom intended, 78
— — infringements of, 15–28
— — limitation of scope by legal
    decisions, 106–10
— — list of, 111–19
— — methods of publication,
    1–3
— — rates in, compared with
    market rates, 22–8
— — types of work covered,
    9–11
— — where recorded, 1–3

Clothworkers, special treatment
    of, 80–6
Cost-of-living aspect, 67–86

Departure, unlawful, 34–8,
    89–101
Detaining of wages, 43–4, 46–52
Dismissal, unlawful, 42–6, 97
Disputes, adjudged by justices,
    44–52

Exactions, excessive, 87–101

Hiring, private, 61–2
— sessions for, 56–65
— yearly, importance of, 62–5

Infringements of wage assess-
    ments, 15–28

Masters, *see* Offences

Offences:
    giving excessive wages, 16–7,
        94–101
    hiring for less than a year,
        64–5
    leaving work unfinished, 34–8,
        89–101
    living idly, 29–34, 89–101
    receiving excessive wages,
        17–8, 94–101
    refusal to serve, 20–2, 29–34,
        89–101
    statute sessions, failure to
        appear at, masters', 58–60
    — — petty constables', 56–8
    — — servants', 61
    testimonials, not producing, 38
    — not requiring production
        of, 38–42
    unlawful departure, 34–8, 89–
        101
    unlawful dismissal, 42–6, 97
    wage assessment offences,
        scarcity of, 18–20
    wage details, not recording,
        58–60
    withholding wages, 43–4,
        46–52
Overpayment, 15–28, 94–101

MADE AND PRINTED IN GREAT BRITAIN BY
EBENEZER BAYLIS AND SON, LTD., THE
TRINITY PRESS, WORCESTER, AND LONDON

For Product Safety Concerns and Information please contact our
EU representative GPSR@taylorandfrancis.com Taylor & Francis
Verlag GmbH, Kaufingerstraße 24, 80331 München, Germany